THE REINCARNATION WORKBOOK

THE REINCARNATION WORKBOOK

A Complete Course in Recalling Past Lives

by

J.H.BRENNAN

THE AQUARIAN PRESS

First published 1989

British Library Cataloguing in Publication Data

Brennan, J. H.
The reincarnation workbook.
1. Psychic phenomena: Reincarnation
I. Title
133.9'01'3

ISBN 0-85030-770-8

The Aquarian Press is part of the Thorsons Publishing Group,
Wellingborough, Northamptonshire, NN8 2RQ, England.

Typeset by Harper Phototypesetters Limited, Northampton
Printed in Great Britain by Woolnough Bookbinding Limited,
Irthlingborough, Northamptonshire

1 3 5 7 9 10 8 6 4 2

For Priscilla M. Jackson, one of the world's great healers,
who may find much of interest in her own past lives some day.

Contents

Introduction

*'It is conceivable that I might be reborn as a Chinese coolie. In such a case
I should lodge a protest.'*

— Sir Winston Churchill

In 1929, something very odd happened to a middle-class couple in Delhi, India.
Their daughter, a three-year-old named Shanti, began to tell them about her
husband and her children. At first, Mr and Mrs Devi paid scant attention. Many
children lead rich fantasy lives and often create imaginary companions. If Shanti
Devi's fantasies were a little adult, a little unusual, it was, in all probability, nothing
to worry about. They felt she would grow out of it and the problem — if it was
indeed a problem — would soon go away.

But it did not go away. Four years later, Shanti was still insisting she had a
husband . . . but now she was filling in the details. His name, she said, was
Kedarnath and she had borne him three children (whom she also named and
described). They had lived together in a town called Muttra where she had died
in 1925 giving birth to a fourth child. It was that last part that worried her parents.
Imaginary husbands and children were all very well — might perhaps even be
expected from a little girl — but Muttra actually existed (it was a town not far
from Delhi) and claims to have died in childbirth sounded alarmingly like some
form of mental illness. They brought Shanti to a doctor.

At this point, the case took the first of many bizarre turns. The doctor listened
carefully to the child's description of her 'death', then told the bewildered parents
it contained medical details which, in his professional opinion, a seven-year-old
child could not possibly know. Nor could he find any reason to conclude she
was mentally ill — which was reassuring, but even more puzzling. For if little
Shanti was not mentally ill, what was happening to her? Where had she found
out so much about death in childbirth? How had she filled in the obscure medical

details? Above all, why did she believe the story she had now told so often? For Shanti herself there was no problem at all. She had, she believed, simply lived before. Her name in her past life had been Ludgi and the details she had given her parents were as she remembered them.

Once again the case took an unusual turn. A business acquaintance of Shanti's father called at the house. Shanti opened the door and recognized him at once as a cousin of her husband. But this claim was more than fantasy. The man did indeed live in Muttra and had a cousin named Kedarnath. Worse still, Kedarnath had had a wife named Ludgi, who died in childbirth. All this, of course, was taking place in India, a country where reincarnation is an act of faith. Despite their earlier scepticism, Shanti's parents were, perhaps, more willing to accept the possibility their daughter could have lived before than a Western couple might have been. Without telling Shanti, they arranged a test. Before long a stranger called at the door. Shanti recognized him without hesitation. She had once again met Kedarnath, the man she claimed as her husband from a previous life.

By now word of these strange developments was spreading. Eventually it spread sufficiently for the Government to take note. Interest created in the case was running so high that an investigative committee was set up. Scientists descended on the hapless child, determined to discover — one way or the other — whether her experiences were genuine.

For the first time in her young life, Shanti visited Muttra. To the astonishment of all concerned, she was so familiar with the town that she was able to lead the researchers through it blindfold! And when the bandage was removed from her eyes, she had no trouble in finding her former home where she recognized and correctly named Kedarnath's father, mother and brother. Kedarnath's children by his deceased wife Ludgi were brought out. Amid scenes of intense emotion, Shanti recognized three of them. The fourth, whom she did not know, was the child born as Ludgi died.

Shanti Devi then took the scientists to the home of Ludgi's mother where she proceeded to point out structural and decorative differences to the house as she remembered it. Ludgi's mother, wary though she was of this strange child with her retinue of scientists, none the less confirmed the changes had all taken place since Ludgi's death. As final proof, Shanti insisted Ludgi had buried some rings before she died and volunteered to show the investigators where they were hidden. The scientists dug where she indicated and did indeed discover a small bag of rings. Ludgi's mother identified them as having belonged to her daughter.

Was Shanti Devi what she claimed to be — the reincarnation of Ludgi, wife of Kedarnath, who had died in childbirth in 1925? The scientific committee who investigated eventually filed a report in which they freely admitted to having found no indications of trickery or fraud. Many more experts have sifted the evidence in the intervening years, still without casting doubt on its veracity.

At about the time Ludgi was dying in childbirth, Bishen Chand, the five-year-old son of railway clerk Ram Ghulam Kapoor, was beginning to discover in himself memories of a past existence. Although no one had yet taught him the facts of life, he started to discuss sex with his amazed (and somewhat embarrassed) father. Like Shanti Devi, Bishen lived in India, in Bareilly, Uttar Pradesh. His memories, it transpired, corresponded eerily to the life of a wealthy ne'er-do-well named

Laxmi Narain, who had died in 1918 at the age of 32. A feature of Laxmi's life was his passion for a prostitute named Padma.

As with Shanti Devi, the question had to be asked: where could a five-year-old find such intimate and adult details of a life which could be verified historically? For Bishen, the question was far from academic. 18 years after he first remembered her, the prostitute Padma walked into the office at Tenakpore where he was working. Bishen was thunderstruck, so overcome by emotion that he fainted. That night he went to her home carrying a bottle of wine in remembrance of Laxmi (although as Bishen he was teetotal) and determined to take up the old relationship where it left off. (Romantics will be disappointed to learn that Padma was having none of it. She pointed out that even if he was Laxmi reincarnate, she was now old enough to be his mother, and sent him home.)

Not all evidence of rebirth derives from long ago and far away, although there does seem to be some tendency for case histories to arise most frequently in cultures sympathetic to the idea of reincarnation.

In 1968, for example, the two-year-old New Delhi child, Reena Gupta, was already claiming to her grandmother that she had a husband . . . who had murdered her! Reena's behaviour soon became as bizarre as her remarkable story. She took to scanning street crowds for her husband and children, of which she believed they had four. She took to criticizing her mother for the way she did the housework and on one occasion even wandered off in the market, following a woman she believed to have visited her home in a previous life.

Into the picture stepped Vijendra Kaur, a colleague of Reena's mother. She had discovered a Sikh couple whose history seemed to coincide with the stories the little girl was telling. The couple, Mr and Mrs Sardar Kishan Singh, were the parents of a woman named Gurdeep Kaur who had been murdered by her husband on 2 June 1961.

The Singhs were intrigued by the news that someone claimed to be their reincarnated daughter and agreed to visit Reena Gupta's home. Reena herself was asleep when they arrived, but awoke to identify them at once as her 'father and mother'.

The following day, Gurdeep's sister Swarna was brought to the Gupta home. Reena not only recognized her, but called her by a family nickname, Sarno. Later Reena was to visit the Singh household where she correctly identified a photograph of Gurdeep, claiming it to be a picture of herself.

Of the many, many case studies in the annals of reincarnation research, this one had by far the most macabre ending. Surjeet Singh, husband and murderer of Gurdeep, was released from jail after serving ten years of a life sentence. He came to hear of Reena's claims and decided to pay her a visit. They met in 1975 when Reena was nine years old and were actually photographed together.

Not all cases are capable of such detailed verification, although circumstantial evidence will often force investigators to take them seriously. Joey Verwey, of Pretoria, South Africa, was three years old when she first recalled what appeared to be past lives. By the time she was six, her mother Helge had begun to keep a careful record of her far memories and continued to do so over the next decade. The case eventually attracted the attention of Dr Arthur Bleksley, who was to profess himself convinced by the evidence. The child, he said, had described objects, manners and fashions of past ages in such minute detail that only reincarnation could explain it.

White South Africa is not, of course, a culture predisposed to belief in reincarnation. But nor is America, where little Romy Crees, three years old in 1981, produced graphic recollections of her life as Joe Williams, a father of three who had met his death in a motor cycling accident. Romy's recollections of this life were as detailed as any example of far memory in the annals of reincarnation research. She recalled going to school in a place called Charles City, living in a red brick house and eventually marrying a woman by the name of Sheila. She recalled that her mother's name was Louise and that she suffered from a pain or injury in her right leg. Although Romy's parents were Roman Catholics with no belief in reincarnation, they realized something unusual was going on and eventually, in desperation, called in the professional researcher Hemendra Banerjee.

There was, some 140 miles distant from Romy's home in Des Moines, Iowa, a small town which bore the name of Charles City. Banerjee decided to take Romy there to see what might develop. The journey was made in 1981. With Romy and Banerjee went Romy's father Barry Crees, Banerjee's wife and research colleague Margit, and a specialist from Des Moines, Dr Greg States. Although Romy had frequently begged to be taken to Charles City, none of them told her where they were going. It seemed, however, she knew perfectly well. As they approached the town she suddenly began to insist they buy her mother blue flowers and mentioned that they would not be able to enter her house through the front door, but would have to 'go round the corner to the door in the middle'.

As Romy had predicted, there was indeed a Mrs Williams living in Charles City, although the prediction itself was not particularly impressive, given that Williams is a fairly common name. But when the party reached the house, they found they could not, in fact, use the front door — the path was blocked by a prominent notice which required them to go round the back.

Mrs Williams, 76 years old and forced to use crutches because of a problem with her right leg, confirmed that she had had a son named Joe, who died in a motorcycle accident near Chicago in 1975 — two years before Romy was born. The house, which was now a white bungalow, had been a red brick building when Joe was young. Joe had married a woman named Sheila and, as Romy claimed, fathered three children. More and more details were confirmed as the encounter proceeded until, in a climax which shattered the elderly Mrs Williams, little Romy recognized a photograph of Joe, Sheila and the children taken within a year of Joe's death.

In the face of these and many similar case histories, we must surely start to re-evaluate some of our most cherished notions of what may happen to us after death. Are we really consigned to Heaven or Hell as many Westerners seem to believe? Do we rot in the grave, patiently awaiting some distant resurrection, as orthodox Christianity teaches? Or is it possible that Oriental ideas are closer to the truth and reincarnation is a fact of life?

Reincarnation is a root creed of both the Hindu and the Buddhist religions. It is found, in one form or another, in the belief structures of many primitive communities. An expanding Roman Empire discovered the doctrine among the

Continental Gauls and the Druids of Britain. Classical sources assure us the Orphics and Pythagoreans of Greece subscribed to it. Although not a tenet of orthodox Judaism, it seems to have influenced a variety of ancient Jewish sects, notably the mystical Essenes and the Pharisees. Some scholars (not to mention St Jerome) held it was an important doctrine of the early Christian Church — a possibility underlined by the fact that the Second Council of Constantinople saw fit to outlaw the belief in AD 553. 'If anyone assert the fabulous pre-existence of souls,' the Bishops declared, 'and shall submit to the monstrous doctrine that follows from it, let him be anathema.'

In 1980, Dr James Parejko of Chicago State University carried out a study and discovered the Bishops are now fighting a rearguard action. 93 per cent of hypnotized volunteers produced apparent recollections of a previous existence. And the best subjects were those who had previously denied belief in reincarnation. But then, of course, reincarnation is no longer a question of *belief*. Serious research into the phenomenon has been going on for years and a mass of evidence has accumulated. Some of the most impressive research has been remarkably *public* British television viewers were entertained just a few years ago by a programme in which a deeply entranced woman recollected her life as a Jewess, fleeing from the pogroms (massacres) in York centuries ago. She took refuge in the crypt of a Christian church . . . a crypt that was rediscovered only *after* the programme was recorded, having been sealed off for hundreds of years.

Something even more dramatic was broadcast to Australian audiences in 1983. Four Sydney housewives were regressed by hypnotist Peter Ramster and the evidence they produced was verified under the watchful eye of the TV cameras. In one instance, the verification process involved a trip to France. There the subject, Cynthia Henderson, led a film crew to the ruin of a 300-year-old Normandy chateau which she had described in colloquial French during her regression experience.

So, if people young and old, from countries East and West can remember their past lives spontaneously, might it not be possible to *induce* similar memories in anyone?

The Reincarnation Workbook is based on the premise that it is, that techniques exist which will permit you to investigate the phenomenon of far memory and judge for yourself how important it might be to your present life. It has been created as a structured study course designed to give you the background knowledge and techniques necessary to

- understand the reincarnation process;

- interpret ancient doctrines in the light of modern knowledge;

- investigate your own past lives and those of relatives or friends;

- use knowledge gained to influence your present life.

The course is built around a series of lessons, each of which is, in turn, divided into two parts. The first part is *theory* and deals with a specific aspect of the reincarnation process. These sections will help you build your understanding of what reincarnation is all about, for research suggests the process is not nearly so straightforward as many people imagine. The second part is *practice* and provides you with the various techniques necessary to investigate past lives.

The practical sections of the first four lessons are unusual in that they deal with methods anyone can apply with absolute certainty of achieving results. These techniques, based on the working hypothesis that reincarnation is a fact, permit you to investigate your present life for clues to your past — a process which will go a long way towards indicating the types of past lives you may have led . . . and where you may have led them.

The remaining lessons are more specialized and in many instances more advanced, both in their theoretical and practical aspects. They may seem a little daunting at first glance, but the results that can be obtained from the methods outlined can be spectacular in the extreme and will well repay the time and effort invested.

Exactly how much time will tend to vary in relation to the lesson. The first four lessons actually form a sort of mini-course in their own right and you may well decide to devote quite a lot of time to them. The work you will put into the remainder must depend on how far you want to go with your research. Should you decide to go all the way, completion of this Workbook will leave you as well equipped as most professional researchers in terms of knowledge and technique. However far you decide to go, proceed at your own pace. This is not a test or competition. There are no examinations at the end. It is a learning process and should not be hurried.

1.

Anatomy of the Soul

*'But **is** there a true self?'*

— Colin Wilson

You would imagine it must be easy to amass self-knowledge. You have lived with yourself all your life. You know everything you ever did — because you were there when you did it. You even have access to what goes on inside your head — you can listen in to all those intimate thoughts and speculations that are hidden from other people. But for all that, amassing self-knowledge is one of the most difficult things in the world. Because however open and transparent you may *seem*, the reality is that you are nothing of the sort. Your inner processes are extremely complex. Huge areas of your mind are capable of hiding themselves from you — *and routinely do so*. In short, you are much more than you imagine.

In modern times, one of the first people to suspect this truth was a Viennese physician named Josef Breuer. Towards the end of the nineteenth century, Breuer found himself treating a 21-year-old patient he referred to in his published records as 'Fraulein Anna O'.

Anna exhibited severe and frightening symptoms. Her sight and speech were seriously disturbed. She could not eat. She suffered from intermittent paralysis. At times the disease — whatever the disease might have been — seemed to affect her brain, for her personality would change from that of an adult to that of a child, indulging in extremes of behaviour.

Anna's bizarre illness struck shortly after the death of her father, a clue that would be more meaningful now than it was then. One day while Anna was telling him the details of a particularly severe episode, Breuer noticed to his amazement that her symptoms gradually disappeared. He began to wonder if she was suffering from a physical illness at all, or whether there was something in her mind that was causing her all the trouble, perhaps as a reaction to her father's death. Breuer followed up this thought by using hypnosis — a fashionable tool among Viennese doctors of his day — and produced an outstandingly successful cure.

In 1882, Breuer met the ambitious young physician Sigmund Freud. Freud, who was then 26, was fascinated by Anna's case history and discussed its details with Breuer over and over again. He was particularly interested in what the patient herself had called 'the talking cure'. At the time, Freud had already met the famous French neurologist Jean Charcot and subsequently tried to interest him in the therapy Breuer had developed. But Charcot was preoccupied with other things.

The encounter was not a total loss, for Charcot demonstrated to Freud that he could use hypnosis to induce tremors, paralysis, anesthesia and a variety of other symptoms. This confirmed what Freud had already suspected: the human mind played a major part in certain types of illness. Later he was to formulate the principle that these '. . . symptoms originate through the energy of the mental process being withheld from conscious influence and being diverted into bodily innervation (conversion)'.

This is not the most lucid statement in the world, but the important part is clear enough. When Freud spoke of certain mental events being *withheld from conscious influence* he was already on the road to his most famous doctrine: the notion that there is more to the mind than meets the eye. Freud soon came to see it as divided into two main areas — the conscious, which is the part you are aware of, and the subconscious, which is just as real, just as important, but hidden.

Oddly enough, Freud did not make his first systematic statement about the subconscious until 1912 when he published an article in the *Proceedings* of the Society for Psychical Research. In it he wrote, 'We obtain our concept of the unconscious from the theory of repression'. In other words, when a thought was pushed out of the conscious mind, it did not disintegrate but continued to exist in the subconscious. To Freud, the subconscious was a sort of dustbin which held the trash thrown out by the more central processes of thought.

I have gone into the historical background in some depth for a reason.

Freud's early model of a two-part mind, conscious and unconscious, is the one in most common use today. It is the way average people think about themselves and it is assumed to be supported by an overwhelming weight of scientific evidence.

But this is not true at all. The model was — and still is — no more than Freud's first halting attempt to account for certain things he had observed. It was a theory among other theories and however popular it may have become, it is not the only possible (and not even the best possible) explanation of a human being's inner processes. Freud himself recognized this and introduced a three-part division of the mind into *id, ego* and *superego*. The id was a little like the subconscious of his early theory — a reservoir of instinctive impulses. The ego was that portion of the id which was influenced by external circumstances and thus equated more or less with the conscious mind. The superego was the seat of our inhibitions. In a less scientific environment it might have been called Conscience.

Freud's early fascination with Breuer's 'talking cure' remained, and he developed it into the famous system of psychoanalysis which is still extremely popular as a therapy today. In psychoanalysis, you are invited to relax, release your inhibitions, and explore the half-forgotten memories of those events which have made you what you are. Since, by definition, a great many such events occurred in childhood, close attention is paid to that area of your life. But memories of childhood are not always easy to dredge up, so that your analyst (if medically qualified) may have to make use of drugs or, as in Freud's own day, hypnosis.

The process of pushing back towards childhood is known by the psychoanalytic term of *regression*. In the therapeutic process of regression, it is considered important that key experiences are not merely remembered, but remembered so vividly their emotional charge is released, a process known as *abreaction*.

Most psychoanalysis is carried out in an attempt to relieve a patient's symptoms — that is to say, as a therapy. The analyst seeks to guide you towards those forgotten experiences which fester in a troublesome manner below the threshold of consciousness. In the practice of psychoanalysis, some analysts theorized that the most troublesome experiences might actually be the very earliest: the moment of birth, for example, when you leave the warmth, peace and security of your mother's womb to plunge into a confusion of light, noise, helplessness and often pain. Such analysts pushed regression to extremes. Their patients reported recall of cradle events and even the birth trauma itself. A few claimed to be able to remember life *within* the womb. And then, though it was not widely publicized, a handful of patients produced more distant memories still. They had recall of lives *beyond* the womb.

Analysts wondered if the respectable process of regression had gone rogue and was producing fantasies or hallucinations. It seemed a likely explanation. Because if the reports of these few patients *were* correct, it would mean they had actually lived before — and that opened up a whole series of scientific and philosophical difficulties, not least of which was that it would require a brand new model of the human mind.

In point of fact, as interest in psychology grew in Freud's Vienna, brand new models of the human mind began to appear all over the place. Although Freud's simplistic subdivision was the one to grip and hold the public imagination, many of his colleagues became convinced it simply would not do. Among them was Carl Jung.

Jung's father was a minister of religion and Jung's psychological make-up that of a visionary. He experienced visitations from a discarnate entity he called *Philemon* which was capable of walking and talking with him in his garden. He had a waking dream of floods of blood shortly before Europe plunged into war. Towards the end of his life, when very ill, he had an out-of-body experience in which his consciousness left the planet. From childhood he had vivid, symbolic dreams.

For anyone with such a rich subjective life, Freud's id/ego/superego subdivision must have seemed a little sterile. Jung's most famous disagreement with his mentor arose out of the importance Freud placed on sex. But it was not just the sexual doctrine which Jung cast aside. He threw away much of Freud's whole basic model of the mind.

Jung replaced it with a new model drawn from one of his own dreams. In this dream, he was in a two-storey house which he somehow knew to be his own. The upper storey was a kind of salon furnished in rococo style with some fine paintings on the walls. It seemed a pleasant place to live, but Jung realized suddenly he did not know what the other storey was like. He descended the stairs and reached the ground floor. There he discovered everything was much older, in a style dating to the fifteenth or sixteenth century. The floors were red brick, the furnishings Medieval, and everywhere was rather dark.

As he continued to explore, he happened on a heavy door. He opened it and found a descending stairway. This took him into a beautifully vaulted chamber with walls of stone block and brick. The architectural style convinced him this portion of the house must be Roman. He examined the stone slab floor and in one of the slabs discovered a ring. In his autobiography, he wrote:

'When I pulled it, the stone slab lifted, and again I saw a stairway of narrow stone steps leading down into the depths. These too I descended and entered a low cave cut into the rock. This dust lay on the floor and in the dust were scattered bones and broken pottery, like remains of a primitive culture. I discovered two human skulls, obviously very old and half disintegrated. Then I awoke.'

It was on this dream that Jung founded what was to become the second most influential model of the human mind, a model still extremely popular with intellectuals and mystics today.

'It was plain to me that the house represented a kind of image of the psyche — that is to say of my then state of consciousness, with hitherto unconscious additions. Consciousness was represented by the salon. It had an inhabited atmosphere, in spite of its antiquated style.

'The ground floor stood for the first level of the unconscious. The deeper I went in, the more alien and darker the scene became. In the cave, I discovered remains of a primitive culture, that is, the world of the primitive man within myself — a world which can scarcely be reached or illuminated by consciousness. The primitive psyche of man borders on the life of the animal soul, just as the caves of prehistoric times were usually inhabited by animals before men laid claim to them.'

In that primitive bottom layer Jung found his most famous postulate — the collective unconscious, a stratum of mental patterns common to us all. Out of the collective unconscious came his theories of archetypes, his insights into alchemy, his fascination with symbols and much more.

We need look no further than Freud and Jung, those two founding fathers of modern psychology, to see the problem that arises time and time again when we examine models of the mind. Psychology is not an exact science and its potential for precise experimentation is strictly limited. Such theories as do arise, tend to be coloured (indeed, *must* be coloured) by the individuals who give them birth. In psychology we have the paradoxical situation of the mind attempting to examine itself, consequently seeing itself through the distorting lenses of its own prejudices and assumptions.

There is little serious argument against this proposition. Freud's fascination with sexuality and his exposition of the Oedipus Complex are now thought to tell us more about Freud's emotional problems and cultural background than about humanity as a whole. Jung's unique insights arose from the study and experience of Jung's unique mind. We should be extremely cautious about accepting their findings uncritically. The real question is how far their individual observations may be relevant to the rest of us.

Certainly there are many cases which do not seem to fit all that well into the consensus model of the mind which has arisen out of the work of men like Freud and Jung. Among them, curiously enough, were the experiences of Jung's own cousin.

While Jung was still a university student at Basle, his 15-year-old cousin (to whom he referred by the initials S.W. in his published reports) began to show signs of multiple personality. In her normal state, the girl was not a striking individual. Jung described her as of mediocre intelligence and having no special gifts. She was shy, hesitant and poorly educated. Physically, she had a pale, unhealthy look. Yet something happened to S.W. so that from time to time she would cease to talk in her usual Swiss dialect and began to use a smooth, assured, literary German. Spirits claimed to speak through her, including her grandfather and a long dead North German noble.

Both the girl and her family appear to have taken these claims seriously. She began to hold regular Sunday evening seances during which she would bring through spirit messages. These seances continued until her early death, from tuberculosis, at the age of 26. She achieved a degree of notoriety as a medium. But if the family and followers took S.W.'s spirits at face value, Jung did not. He was convinced he was listening to aspects of the girl's own personality.

The trouble with this, of course, was that the girl's own personality was profoundly impoverished when compared with some of those which manifested through her. Jung's notion involved the paradox of a part that was greater than the whole. In retrospect, it looks as though we may be talking less about aspects or fragments of a single personality than about a collection of personalities occupying a single body.

Jung's cousin was certainly not unique in this respect. In 1811, a Pennsylvania woman named Mary Reynolds fell into a deep sleep lasting almost 20 hours. When she woke up, she remembered nothing of her identity or even the language she had spoken and had to relearn everything from scratch, like a child — except that the process took only a few weeks. Just over a month later, she arose one morning to take up her old life exactly where she had left it off. For the next 16 years, two totally different personalities alternated in her body until, eventually, one became more or less dominant up to her death at the age of 62.

If Mary Reynolds had two personalities, Doris Fischer had five. They were studied by the Pittsburgh psychiatrist Walter F. Prince from 1910 onwards. Once again, there was little to suggest Doris Fischer was exhibiting aspects of a single personality: what was clearly presented was a case of several very different people occupying the same body.

The Fischer personalities represent only one among very many similar case studies, carefully investigated and reported over the past century. So commonplace is multiple personality, in fact, that it has given rise to theories of possession in virtually every human culture. Prince wrote about the Doris Fischer case in the *Journal of Abnormal Psychology* in 1916 and there is a very real temptation to assume this is exactly where it belongs. But is the sort of thing Doris Fischer experienced actually abnormal, or is it simply a more exaggerated form of something we all experience?

If you look back over the course of your life, you tend to see yourself as a single individual. But a little thought soon shows this is not exactly the case. You are a very different personality today than you were at, for example, the age of three months. You might even be prepared to admit you are a very different person today than you were in your teens. The older you get, the more these changes become apparent. When I tell you I am not the man I used to be, I speak no more than the sober truth.

Once you begin to examine yourself and your life history with real care and attention, the picture that emerges is not so much a single individual progressing through a series of experiences, but rather a whole daisy chain of linked personalities. I am not, of course, suggesting you exhibit multiple personalities in the way that Doris Fischer did. But it certainly does seem as though, in the course of a life, the current personality is gradually *replaced* by another in an ongoing series of changes, as tenants might succeed each other in a rented house.

But the question of 'multiple personalities' is not confined to the ageing process. The phrase *I don't know what got into me* has become a cliché of the language precisely because it describes something we have all experienced; a situation in which, inexplicably, we find ourselves behaving totally out of character. It is as if, for a short time, some other individual took control of our actions. Of course we don't *really* imagine something got into us — the cliché refers to old theories of possession. But we do, quite often, find it difficult to explain our actions in terms of what we consider to be our essential personality.

There are other, more subtle, examples of the same phenomenon. Any policeman will confirm that if there are half a dozen witnesses to a bank robbery, there will be six different descriptions of the robber. This may no more than underline how unobservant people are, but strangely enough something very similar happens when you ask a variety of witnesses to describe an individual they all know extremely well. In this latter instance, the physical descriptions will largely coincide, but descriptions of the personality will often vary — sometimes to an astonishing degree.

It may seem trite to remark that a wife will see her husband very differently to the way he is seen by his employees, his business partner or his parents. But are the differences only variations in perception, the same object viewed from different angles? Or are they something else, something perhaps a little deeper, more profound?

In discussing this question with colleagues, I was alerted to the interesting theory that different people *call up* different personalities within us. Thus it is not that your mother sees you differently to the way your employer sees you, but that you actually *become* a different person when you relate to her. This is a most intriguing suggestion; and one which certainly seems to fit common observation. It is at its most obvious at its most extreme. To much of the world Hitler was a genocidal monster. To the Nazi Party he was a bold, determined leader. To Eva Braun he was a gentle, middle-class fiance who loved children, liked dogs and enjoyed cream cakes with his tea. These perceptions are so much at variance it is almost easier to suggest three individuals inhabiting Hitler's body than to accept them as simply different viewpoints of the same man.

And if the theory seems to fit the facts when you look outwards, it is even more impressive when seen from the inside. You know, of course, that you feel differently in the company of different people. There are some with whom you relax, some who make you tense, some with whom you are secretive, others with whom you are open. For most of us, the recognition that we *feel* different is about as far as it goes. But even a little self-examination will show you actually *behave* quite differently, depending on the company you keep. You are (hopefully) far more loving towards your spouse than your boss. You are stiffer, more cautious, when questioned by a policeman than when you deal with a hamburger salesman. The homely examples are deliberately chosen to show that alternating personalities are not something alien, something distant from us, something properly relegated to the *Journal of Abnormal Psychology*. They form part of our day-to-day existence and it is only in their more extreme, exaggerated form that they become a pathology.

A funny, fascinating novel called *The Dice Man* was written in the 1970s by an author named Luke Rhinehart. In it, the central character, a psychiatrist, reached the conclusion that human personality is not singular, but that each of us, like the biblical demons, is legion.

In the novel it was postulated that we have one favourite or dominant personality which tends to keep the others in check. Rhinehart went on to suggest that individual growth depends on releasing the subsidiary personalities from bondage and thus his central character proceeded to do using a six-sided die. At regular intervals throughout his day, he would roll the die. His score would then determine which of his multiple personalities took over during the next time period.

Whether or not it would be a good thing to give equal time to what are currently subsidiary personalities is very much open to question (even Rhinehart's fictional psychiatrist got into a great deal of trouble doing it) but self observation may convince you the central premise is valid enough. We really *are* legion, you and I, and any realistic model of the mind must take the fact into account.

On the face of things none of this would seem to have much to do with reincarnation. But that is not altogether true. Until you develop an accurate picture of your soul, you have very little chance of understanding reincarnation. It is probably fair to suggest that a majority of those who actively believe in reincarnation have a distorted — or downright inaccurate — idea of its mechanics. It is possible to live with this quite comfortably so long as reincarnation remains an abstraction. But once you start investigating your own past lives, once you consider *using* reincarnation in an immediate, practical way, you need to see things more clearly.

For more than 20 years, I have invested a great deal of time and energy in the investigation of reincarnation. In that time, one thing has been made very clear to me: There is a vast difference between the *intellectual acceptance* of reincarnation as a theory or belief and the *experience* of past life recall. At worst, the former is uncomfortable. The latter can be shattering.

The problem arises from the fact that we approach life carrying a collection of inbuilt expectations. If you are a product of western culture, your expectations simply do not include the fact that you have lived before . . . and very likely will live again. You may believe it possible. You may even accept it as a fact. But you do not expect it to impinge on your day. As someone put it in a different context, many people believe in angels, but very few expect to meet one in the bus.

When reincarnation *does* impinge, as happens spontaneously to some people and will almost certainly happen to you if you persevere with this course, it is as well to be prepared. One colleague of mine spent more than six months in an agonizingly difficult reappraisal of her personal philosophy following a breakthrough of far memory. I believe it to be better — and I *know* it is more comfortable — to begin that type of reappraisal *before* the roof falls in.

The place to start is the way you see yourself. If we began this lesson by remarking that self-knowledge is one of the most difficult things in the world, it is also one of the most important — and doubly so if you are seriously determined to begin investigating your past lives. It is always easy to accept the experts, to quote Freud, or Jung, or Adler, Skinner, Pavlov or the hundred and one other famous theorists. But you cannot be certain any one of them is right, or that their findings, even if *generally* correct, are relevant to your own case.

In a relatively short time, you will begin to undergo some of the strangest experiences of your entire life. These experiences can enrich you profoundly, but they can also cause you great emotional pain and substantial intellectual confusion.

I would spare you both.

Lesson One

In this Introduction to this Workbook are details of a variety of case histories in which individuals began, spontaneously, to remember past lives. It is possible to *stimulate* such memories. And the key to doing so is your own imagination.

In this and the next three lessons, you will be shown how to use your imagination in a certain way, then analyse the results for past life clues. Any conclusions you come to will have to be filed away as unproven at this stage, but later in the course you will learn how to go about verifying them.

To break you in gently, your first task is very simple and straightforward: go out and buy yourself a notebook. Make it a big one, because you will be using it right the way through the course.

In that notebook, first note down, briefly, your own ideas about:

a) The structure of the human mind, and

b) Your perception of the reincarnation process.

Don't spend too much time on either. No one is looking for an essay — just a few notes that will act as a touchstone for you in the months ahead.

Next, devote a little time to an important act of imagination. Try to imagine how you would feel, how you would react, if you were given absolute, conclusive proof that you had lived before. In particular, try to work out what changes you would have to make in your philosophy — and possibly even lifestyle — as a result of the knowledge.

None of this need (or should) take you a great deal of time. What comes next may take longer, but the harder you are prepared to work at it the better results you will get. Because what comes next is your first step towards awakening far memories.

Start by answering this question:

If you could win an all-expenses-paid trip to any country in the world, where would you most like to go?

....

Write down your answer in the space provided. Don't let practical considerations come into it. Imagine you can get lots of time off from your job, travelling will be worry-free and all your expenses will be taken care of. All *you* have to do is select your destination.

Once you have written in your answer, close your eyes and try to imagine what you would find there. **Don't** go running for the nearest reference book. Accuracy is not the point. What we are looking for is what you would *expect* to find.

Try to make this as wide-ranging as possible. Think about the sort of places you would expect to see, the sort of people you would expect to meet. Think in terms of smells, of colours, music, moods. Try to imagine typical architecture, typical furnishings, typical craftwork, art, ornamentation.

Don't rush it. Take as much time as you need and spread the whole exercise over as many sessions as you need. At the end of each session, jot down your expectations in your notebook under the heading of the country you selected. There is no need to go into exhaustive detail with this record, but make sure to note the salient points as memory prompters.

When you have done all this, complete the brief Questionnaire below:

Questionnaire

1. Have you ever read any stories, fact or fiction, about your selected destination? If so, name any you remember that stood out.

....

....

....

....

2. Do you enjoy watching movies or TV programmes about your selected destination? Again, name any that stood out.

....

....

....

....

3. Do you happen to know anybody from that country? (Or anybody who has lived there for more than six months?) If so, try to describe your feelings towards them.

....

....

....

....

4. What foods do you associate with your selected destination? Have you ever tasted them . . . and do you like them?

....

....

....

....

5. List any particularly strong feelings (positive or negative) you may have experienced when you were imagining your selected destination.

....

....

....

....

6. Do you have anything in your home — furnishings, rugs, ornaments, pictures etc. — which remind you of your selected destination for any reason? If so, list them.

....

....

....

....

When you have completed the Questionnaire, return to your notebook and take as much time and space as you need to write a *fictional* account of the sort of person you might have been had you lived a past life in your selected destination. Take time to make this as detailed as possible, noting things like the period in which you might have lived, the sort of clothes you wore, the sort of house you lived in and so on. **Do not** — and this is very important — do any research for your story. Each and every detail must be drawn from your imagination *only*.

When you have finished, go on to the next chapter.

2.

The Reincarnation Process

'The Oversoul is before Time.'

— Ralph Waldo Emerson

What is the *real* structure of the human mind? It is entirely possible this question may be unanswerable. In physics, observation of certain particles changes the way they behave. One suspects that observation of the mind might do the same, especially since, as we noted earlier, we are talking about the mind observing itself. But if we may never know its ultimate structure, we can certainly examine *aspects* of that structure as they relate to reincarnation. A good place to start is with Carl Jung's cousin.

You will recall from Chapter 1 that the unfortunate S.W. developed what we would loosely call mediumistic powers in her early teens, that these powers allowed 'spirits' to speak through her and that Jung considered he was actually listening to the voices of S.W.'s own multiple personalities. One of these personalities manifested as a mature, even saintly, individual calling itself *Ivenes*. In sharp contrast to what Jung knew of his cousin's mundane personality, Ivenes presented herself as highly intelligent, confident and self-possessed. She also claimed to be the *real* S.W.

This is an interesting development. In later years, Jung was to speculate that S.W. somehow knew, at an unconscious level, that she was destined to die young and that the Ivenes personality was an attempt to compensate for her lack of maturity. Which is all very well — and may even be true — but does not explain how a shy, hesitant, unintelligent and poorly educated teenager could create such a personality out of thin air and, apparently, overnight.

The notion of a mature and powerful personality hidden within us does not stand or fall with the case of S.W. The psychologist Pierre Janet cites the case of Leonie, a peasant woman who had been subject to attacks of somnambulism in childhood. Under hypnosis, a second personality emerged, more lively and vital than the first, which flatly denied being the same person as the waking Leonie. Leonie 2 actually considered Leonie 1 to be stupid. This is intriguing enough, but as time went by a third personality, Leonie 3, emerged. Leonie 3 was both different and superior to either of the others. She thought of Leonie 1 as a good, but essentially stupid, woman and Leonie 2 as a crazy creature.

Here too the same problem arises as with S.W. It is possible to view Leonie 2 as a sort of negative image of Leonie 1, lively where she was quiet, bright where she was dull. Such a supposition would make good orthodox psychological sense in that we could easily imagine Leonie 2 as comprising those personality aspects which Leonie had been forced to suppress due to the pressures of her peasant existence. But Leonie 3 is far harder to explain. You find yourself wondering where a simple peasant found the building blocks to construct her.

Dr Prince noted that the various personalities which manifested in the Doris Fischer case were definitely ranked in a sort of hierarchy which ranged from a very primitive entity at the bottom all the way up to a supposed spirit who claimed to have come in answer to the prayers of Doris's dead mother. The lowest ranked personality was little more than a memory bank. When she manifested, the body of Doris Fischer was able to relay, word for word, conversations which had occurred years before. These conversations were accompanied by the vocal tones, emotional responses and facial expressions of the original Doris as she had been at the time they took place. But it was fairly evident that the personality through which these memories came, scarcely understood what was going on around her. The supposed spirit at the top of the hierarchy was, by contrast, described by Prince as 'the maturest, wisest and most prescient of the quintet'. It seemed to know more than the others and, to some extent, had control over them.

The same hierarchical structure can be seen in the psyche of Sybil Dorsett, one of the most extreme cases of multiple personality on record, manifesting no fewer than 16 separate personalities within her. Sybil seems to have developed (if that is really the correct word) her inner host in reaction to extreme ill-treatment by her mother. But the personalities themselves were among the most impressive ever studied. They included a builder, a carpenter, a writer, a musician and a painter. The separate, rounded nature of each personality is emphasized by the fact that the writer and the musician became firm friends, manifesting together in Sybil's body in order to hold conversations or attend plays and concerts. One other of the series, a mature woman who called herself Vicky, stood at or near the top of the hierarchy and often looked after the others. On one occasion she prevented Sybil committing suicide by throwing herself in the Hudson River.

Once again it is important to note that while we have been studying pathological manifestations of multiple personality, there is considerable evidence to suggest that these are no more than exaggerated examples of something inherent in us all. The founder of Transactional Analysis, Dr Eric Berne, based his entire system on the theory that even the healthiest human mind has within itself not one personality but three — whom he described as the Parent, the Adult and the Child.

Berne noted that varying circumstances could make one or other of these personalities dominant, but the phenomenon of switching is so universal that it is scarcely ever noticed in normal social intercourse. Until, that is, you begin to look for it. Once you have become sensitized to Berne's notion of Parent/Adult/Child, it is relatively easy to watch it happening in those around us; and in ourselves. Observation confirms Berne's descriptions are apt. When the Child manifests, not only do behaviour patterns change, but very often *voice* patterns do as well.

Berne theorized that the three fundamental personalities within us are *constructs* — that is to say, they are not inherent, but built up in response to experience. The Parent, for example, is a sort of semi-fictional creation based on the nature of the parent of the same sex as ourselves. But if we look beyond Berne to the cases we have already considered, the idea of constructs seems altogether less tenable. It is almost impossible to read of Sybil's writer and musician attending plays together without thinking of them as entirely separate individuals in their own right. We may pay lip service to modern psychology, but our whole instinct, our whole inclination, is to see Sybil as *possessed*.

This is, of course, precisely how humanity *has* seen the phenomenon since ancient times. The notion that multiple personalities are no more than fragments of a shattered psyche is a very recent invention. And it is an invention that does not hold up that well.

The pseudonymous author of *Hook Operators and Things*, a fascinating first-person account of the onset, development and cure of schizophrenia, tells how something in her looked after her while she was at the worst phase of her disease. At a time when she was prey to the most fearsome hallucinations, this secondary personality ensured she stayed out of trouble, and remained reasonably comfortable and well fed. On one remarkable occasion, it appears to have used some form of psychical ability to enable her to win some very necessary money in a gambling casino. In this case, we have a 'personality fragment' which appears to function far more effectively than the sick whole.

Religious literature and the mythologies of almost every race on earth propose the notion of Guardians, supernatural entities whose job it is to look after individual human beings. Most cultures speak of Guardian Spirits, sometimes insisting (rather like Dr Berne) that they are the shades of dead parents or other ancestors. In Moslem and Christian communities, the Guardian is more often thought to be a Guardian Angel, a winged creature who stands behind your right shoulder, whispering with the voice of conscience and (albeit rarely) intervening to save you from disaster.

That such entities were thought of as something a great deal more than pious myth is borne out by the experience of the eccentric Victorian scholar, S.L. MacGregor Mathers. Towards the end of the nineteenth century, Mathers translated a fifteenth century esoteric manuscript to find it contained detailed and explicit instructions for 'obtaining the knowledge and conversation of your Holy Guardian Angel'. These instructions formed a six-month-long practice of religious yoga, including strict regimes of fasting, bathing, purification and prayer. They were a practical approach to an unusual goal and one which some modern exponents of the system claim still works.

In this context, it is worth remarking that the magical practice of every country on earth contains instructions for the invocation of spirit beings. As we watch the special-effects spirits manifest hideously in the latest horror film, it is easy to forget there is an important difference between the terms *invocation* and *evocation*. Evocation, which is the sort of thing we watch in the horror movies, is the supposed art of causing supernatural entities to take on objective visible appearance. Invocation, by contrast, is the art of causing those same beings to manifest *within yourself*.

Whether or not such techniques work in any practical sense is not the point here. The point is only that a great many people, over a very long period of time, have been aware of what we now call multiple personalities, have recognized that they can manifest within a human mind, but consider them entirely separate entities, distinct from their host and complete in themselves.

This is no longer a fashionable idea, but I have reason to believe it is still well worth consideration. It is unfortunate that, as we have already noted, most modern studies of multiple personality arise out of pathological conditions. Every one of the eminent medical investigators so far mentioned has assumed that the multiple personalities were *created* by the pathology. They were seen as psychic fragments, as pseudo-personalities masquerading as the real thing. This assumption leads directly to the view of multiple personalities as *symptoms*. Where they are found to be present (except as the watered-down constructs of Transactional theory) they are held to be indicators of mental illness.

But this is a blinkered view. It ignores the plain fact that there are a great many people manifesting multiple personalities, who show no (other) indication of mental illness. Carl Jung, with his Philemon figure, was one of them. Unless we are prepared to define the appearance of multiple personalities as a mental illness in itself, we are forced to admit that while multiple personalities may be present in certain pathological conditions, they are not necessarily either cause or symptom.

Unfortunately, this step leads us at once into deep water (which, I suspect, is why so few people care to take it). If multiple personalities are *not* manifestations of insanity, what are they? Surely we should not be forced back to the whole Medieval concept of possession with its attendant ragbag of angels and demons, heaven and hell?

It seems to me the only honest answer to this question is *not exactly*. I have had the good fortune to be able to study one major and several minor examples of multiple personality at first hand. In none of these cases were the host individuals mentally ill, nor were they 'possessed' in the traditional sense of the word. They functioned effectively and normally in what we like to call the real world and in at least one of the cases drew substantial benefit from co-operation with the secondary entity.

My observation of these cases led me to conclude that in some instances the secondary personalities *were* constructs — slightly more sophisticated and less predictable constructs than those outlined by Dr Berne, but constructs all the same. They seemed essentially to be masks donned by the individual in order to meet the demands of certain situations, or as a response to certain stimuli.

Often, these constructs would *behave* like separate individuals, they would act without the volition of their host, sometimes in ways their host would not have wished. But as a novelist, I am perfectly familiar with constructs behaving in just this way. It is a cliché of fiction writing that strongly drawn characters have a habit of going their own way . . . and making mincemeat of your plotline in the process. Several secondary personalities I have studied are exactly like that: fictional characters living not on the printed page, but within the psyches of their creators. In one important case, however, I am absolutely satisfied that an entirely different mechanism was (and still is) at work. Here the secondary personality was not created by its host, but *bequeathed* to her by a friend whose body it had shared for many years.

This is a bizarre situation and one difficult to describe lucidly. I find myself unhappy with terms like *secondary*, which suggests second class, and even *it* which suggests a thing, while the reality was very much a rounded, intelligent *person* lacking only a body of its own to make him the sort of friend you would be proud to introduce at a party.

I do not know where this discarnate individual — for convenience we may call him Paul — actually originated. He claims to have functioned in Palestine at the time of Christ and earlier in ancient Egypt, but I have found no way to check this out. What I do know is that Paul shared the mind of an Englishman interested in the occult, who passed him on to a favoured female pupil shortly before he (the Englishman) died. Paul has remained a sort of sleeping partner to the woman ever since, quiescent for much of the time, but appearing every now and then to talk with her, or with others, using her vocal chords. He is able, routinely, to supply her with information — usually historical — of which she had no prior knowledge. On one occasion he demonstrated his ability to set up temporary communication within the mind of a third party.

If this is some sort of personality fragment at work, it is certainly not behaving as it should. Everything about Paul, particularly his memory, access to information and apparent freedom of movement from body to body, strongly suggests a true individual, completely independent from his hosts. In this sense, he fits the theory of spirits so widely held throughout human history. But then fictional creations behave, in many respects, like spirits too.

This latter point has been highlighted by the Toronto Society for Psychical Research, which experimentally *created* a ghost called Philip. This was done exactly as an author creates a character, but in a group context. The difference was that when the job was done, Philip began to communicate with the group as spirits have done at seances for centuries.

There is considerable similarity between this case and the technique of *tulpa* creation in Tibet, as reported by that intrepid traveller Madame Alexandra David-Neel. Practitioners of this technique visualize an entity so strongly that it takes on a literal life of its own. Madame David-Neel, who learned the technique from lamas, experimented with it so successfully that her creation was eventually *seen by other members of her party*.

As you expand your knowledge of cases of this type, the result is less likely to be enlightenment than confusion. Entities running round inside the human head seem sometimes to be independent, sometimes to be fictional creations, and sometimes both . . . when, that is, they are not exactly what psychiatrists claim them to be: fragmented aspects of the host's own personality.

What is urgently needed here is a new model of the mind which is sufficiently flexible to encompass these various observations. Since I have yet to find one suitable available for purchase off the shelf, I propose to create my own:

The human psyche is a field phenomenon. The totality of your mind functions far more like a place than a state. It is a place inhabited by that node of consciousness which makes up your central awareness — and by a variety of other individuals as well!

Certain of these individuals are your direct creation, tulpas of the mind. Others are visitors from outside. Still others are your indirect *creation (a point we shall return to in a moment) and form links in a chain which is itself the totality of your being.*

Most times, these multiple personalities behave like the most courteous of guests, moving about discreetly in the background and taking great care not to make too much noise. Occasionally, however, something turns these guests into rebels and they try to move into a more central position, or even take over the whole mind/body complex — an act which creates the conditions we interpret as possession or pathology.

I put forward this model not as some ultimate truth, but in the hope that it may prove useful to you when you come to evaluate the phenomena generated by your reincarnation studies. For all this has far more to do with reincarnation than might be immediately apparent. The linkage appears once we ask ourselves where these inner entities come from. For some, of course, the pedigree is easy enough to trace. But others remain a mystery. They seem never to have been born; and where they do not manifest through a living human mind, there is no information available about where they live.

Ivenes, the mature and powerful personality who manifested through Carl Jung's cousin, propounded a very curious doctrine to those who attended the weekly seances. S.W., she said, was only the latest of a series of incarnations. She had lived before at the time of Nero, when she was a Christian martyr. She has also been a French countess burned as a witch, a cleric's wife and a seeress.

When I first read of this suggestion by Ivenes, it rang familiar bells. For exactly the same picture had emerged quite independently from my own reincarnation research. Using hypnosis and other trance techniques, I was able to push subjects to examine some fundamental structures of their psyches. The picture that emerged was a far cry from Freud's id/ego/superego trinity and even differed — at least in emphasis — to the mental model I created a short time ago as a helpful hypothesis for anyone engaged in reincarnation research. What emerged was this:

You have a central essence which is non-material, exceptionally enduring (possibly even immortal) and has existed in some alien plane or dimension for thousands of years before your present life.

While this entity is the fundamental you, it is obviously far more experienced than the familiar you of everyday consciousness. The Little You, if I may use that term, has lived at most for ninety or so years. The Big You ('out there') has the experience of many thousands of years to draw upon.

The way the Big You has gained this experience has everything to do with what we normally think of as reincarnation. It creates personalities as the focus of its attention. Such personalities are 'sent' into incarnation to learn and experience. On physical death, the personality is withdrawn and the sum of its experience absorbed into the pre-existent entity which gave it birth.

Those of you who indulge in Fantasy Role Playing games will have little difficulty understanding this picture. In FRP, you create characters who engage in adventures according to the rules of the role play system you are using. The adventures take place in a world you create by an act of imagination. Fantasy Role Play is popular because imaginary adventures of this type are extremely vivid. The created characters 'come alive' in much the same way as those of a novelist. But the whole process of role play is one in which *you*, an entity existing *outside* the adventure world and living a great deal longer than any of the characters within it, create personalities which permit you to experience the adventure, if not exactly first hand, at least in a most enjoyable, entertaining and sometimes even educational manner.

Others have, of course, hit on the discovery of the *Big You* before now, usually referring to it more elegantly than I do. The writer on esoteric subjects, Manly P. Hall, showed he was conversant with the theory when he commented, 'Suicide thwarts the plan of the entity *which sends out the personality*' (italics mine).

When asked about reincarnation, the spirit guide Silver Birch remarked, 'There is reincarnation, but not in the same sense in which it is generally expounded. There is in our (spirit) world a spiritual diamond which has many, many facets. These come into your world to gain experience and to add their quota to the diamond's lustre and brilliance. Thus the personalities that are incarnated are facets of the one individuality'.

In the opening of his book *Past Lives*, John Van Auken writes: 'The idea that you and I have reincarnated is somewhat of a misconception. The 'you' and 'I' that we consider to be our normal, everyday selves has actually *not* reincarnated . . . However, there is an *inner* part of us that *has* been alive before. This part has incarnated in the Earth's dimension many times.'

If you think about this, some important insights arise. One is that you no longer view reincarnation as a process by which you bounce from one life to another like a rubber ball. Rather it is a process by which a *pre-existent* entity, which has its existence outside of time and space, experiences life by dipping various personalities in the timestream at different intervals.

Another insight is that the nature of time may be such that the various personalities are actually *coexistent*, especially if you take the Big You viewpoint. But whether they are or not, it is easy to see the picture is one of you not as a single individual, but as an interlinked series of reincarnated personalities.

It is important that you are aware of concepts like that of the pre-existent you and the daisy chain of interlinking personalities, because I strongly suspect they will both arise spontaneously in the course of your own research. Indeed, I half suspect most of the techniques given in this course actually help you to study those linked personalities *as they manifest in the deeper levels of your psyche*. In other words, they put you in closer communication with what I have called the Big You and what others have called the Guardian who ultimately controls your destiny.

Lesson Two

There are two ways you can carry out reincarnation research — on other people, or on yourself. Using other people is certainly interesting, sometimes fascinating, but as you began to find out in the last lesson, there is nothing to beat finding out what *you* used to be.

Once you begin to understand the mechanics of reincarnation, you quickly come to realize the information is all in there, locked up in the deeper strata of your mind. Your only real problem is reaching it.

Your practical work for Lesson One began the process of reaching it. Creative fantasy does not produce something out of nothing. Rather it looks for raw material and reworks it or simply dusts it off and re-presents it. By allowing your mind to roam freely, you opened up channels through which information might, potentially, flow. Whether the material you have already recorded in your notebook represents genuine past life recall is something you will have to investigate at a later date. For the moment, it is enough to gather and record clues.

Your main task for this lesson is similar in many ways to the exercise you carried out for the last. But before we come to it, I want to add a technique which will not alone help you with this lesson's exercise, but will be increasingly important to you as you move through the remainder of the course.

Starting tomorrow morning and continuing each morning thereafter, I would like you to set aside a short period for the practice of relaxation. How much time you spend is largely up to you — I don't know how busy your schedule is these days. But you will quickly find that anything less than 10 minutes is not really worthwhile; and I positively do not want you to spend more than half an hour unless you are experienced in the art.

You will need privacy. This is one reason for selecting morning time — if you get up early enough, nobody else will be about. Try to find somewhere where you will not be disturbed, by people, pets or ringing phones. Lock the door if you need to; and if you are particularly sensitive to noise, use earplugs.

Conduct your relaxation session in an upright chair. Don't lie down on a couch or bed: you are far too likely to fall asleep. Begin by regulating your breathing. Relaxation is a physical function. Your muscles use oxygen extracted from your bloodstream. Your bloodstream, in turn, extracts that oxygen from the air you breathe. By regulating your breathing, you increase the oxygen available in your blood, your muscles extract the optimum amount and are far happier to relax for you than they might otherwise be.

If you have studied yoga, you will know there are all sorts of complex breath-regulation techniques. But the one I want you to try is very simple. It is called 2/4 breathing:

1. Breathe *in* to the mental count of four;

2. Hold your breath *in* to the mental count of two;

3. Breathe *out* to the mental count of four;

4. Hold your breath *out* to the mental count of two.

It sounds simple — and it is, although I should warn you there is a bit of a knack to getting it right. (You will know you *have* got it right, incidentally, when you begin doing it without thinking.)

The *rate* at which you should count varies from individual to individual. Start by synchronizing it with your heartbeat. If this doesn't work, play around until you hit on the rhythm that is most comfortable for you.

Get your breathing comfortable before you go on to the second part of the exercise. It is perfectly okay for you to devote an entire session — or a whole year of sessions — to getting your breathing comfortable.

Once you have established a comfortable rhythm of 2/4 breathing, let it run for about three minutes, then start the following relaxation sequence. (If you can hold the 2/4 rhythm while you do it, that's great, but chances are you will not be able to do so at first. In this latter case, just start your session with three minutes of 2/4 breathing, then go back to normal breathing while you carry out the main relaxation sequence, then take up 2/4 breathing again when you are nicely relaxed.)

1. Concentrate on your feet. Wiggle them about. Curl them to tense the muscles, then allow them to relax.

2. Concentrate next on your calf muscles. Tighten and relax them.

3. Concentrate on your thigh muscles. Tighten and relax them.

4. Concentrate on your buttock muscles. Tighten your buttocks and anus, then relax them.

5. Concentrate on your stomach muscles, a very common tension focus. Tighten then relax them.

6. Concentrate on your hands. Curl them into fists, then relax them.

7. Concentrate on your arms. Tighten them rigidly, then relax them.

8. Concentrate on your back. Tighten the muscles, then relax them.

9. Concentrate on your chest. Tighten the muscles, then relax them.

10. Concentrate on your shoulders, another very common tension focus. Hunch your shoulders to tighten the muscles, then relax them.

11. Concentrate on your neck. Tighten the muscles then relax them.

12. Concentrate on your face. Grit your teeth and contort your features to tense up the facial muscles then relax them.

13. Concentrate on your scalp. Tighten the scalp muscles, then relax them.

14. Now tighten up every muscle in your body, holding your entire body momentarily rigid, then relax, letting go as completely as you are able. Do this final whole body sequence again, then again — three times in all. On the third time, take a really deep breath when you tense the muscles and *sigh deeply* aloud as you let the tension go.

15. You should be feeling nicely relaxed by now. If you abandoned your 2/4 breathing at the start of the relaxation sequence, pick it up again at this point.

16. Close your eyes and try to imagine your whole body getting heavier and heavier, as if it were turning to lead. You will find your visualization increases your level of relaxation still further.

Enjoy the sensation of relaxation for the remainder of your session. But stay vigilant. Should you find tension creeping in anywhere (and you certainly will in the early days) don't let it worry you. Just tighten up the tense muscles a little more, then relax them.

I don't know how long it will take you to get the hang of this technique, but I do know the important thing is regular daily practice. Certainly you should be feeling some benefit inside a week and you may be quite proficient in two.

Use the technique regularly until you have trained yourself to relax totally any time you want to.

This may take several months, but don't let that worry you. The important thing is that you have made a start and are determined to continue practising the technique until you are proficient. Once you have made the start on conscious relaxation, you can start in on your next memory stimulation exercise, which covers something ignored in lesson one. In that lesson, you were invited to search for past life memories anywhere in the world. But chances are the one place you never dreamed of looking was right here at home.

Past lives are not always located in some exotic foreign clime. The possibility always arises that you have reincarnated more than once in the same country. It is that possibility you should consider now.

Go through your relaxation exercise so that all tensions have been drained away, then answer the following question:

What district, village, town, city or other location of your native country would you most like to visit?

....

The term 'native country' should be taken to mean the country in which you are living now (or have lived for most of your life) and not necessarily the country where you were actually born.

Your selected location may be somewhere you have already visited, or somewhere you have never been before. When you have made your choice, complete the Questionnaire below:

Questionnaire

1. What feelings, positive or negative, do you experience when you think of that part of your country?

....

....

....

....

2. If you have not already visited this area, what do you expect to find there? Allow your mind to range freely so that it is NOT confined to things about the district you already know.

....

....

....

....

3. Do you associate a certain type of person with this area? If so, what are your feelings, negative or positive, towards that sort of person?

....

....

....

....

When you have filled in your answers, turn back to your notebook. Imagine yourself actually visiting your selected location (either for the first time, or for a return trip if you have already visited in actuality). As you visit, imagine that some object, sight or experience triggers a memory of a past life.

Note down what you imagine that past life would have been; and also note down the imaginary event or object that triggered it. Remember that at this stage you are creating *fiction*, so let your mind run free.

When you have finished, proceed to the next chapter.

3.

Past-Life Influence

'You have inherited most from yourself, not from your family.'
— Edgar Cayce

The possibility that you are actually an immaterial entity, wiser, longer-lived, more powerful than you imagined, may be of purely academic interest to you in this life. But your series of past lives is not. There is substantial evidence that the way you are now, the way you think and react, the whole pattern of your life, may be profoundly influenced by the way you *were*. Surprisingly, the mechanics of this influence are quite well known.

In the early years of the 1914—1918 War, military doctors found themselves coping increasingly with a new kind of casualty, soldiers who, while they had not necessarily suffered any *physical* injury, were unable to function in a normal manner. Since most casualties of this type were victims of trench warfare, it was at first theorized that the noise of artillery shells bursting near them had produced a sort of concussion of the brain. The condition became known as 'shell-shock'. But it was soon evident that the facile explanation would not do. Shell-shock, it transpired, had nothing in common with concussion and often little to do directly with artillery shells. It was a *psychological* condition which arose when an individual successfully forgot a particularly traumatic battlefield experience.

It is human nature to put aside unpleasantness. Most adults will assure you that their schooldays, in the words of the old cliché, were the happiest of their life, despite the fact that manifestly they were nothing of the sort. Old people in particular remember the summers of their childhood as being warmer and drier than they are now, despite the fact that the weather pattern has not changed appreciably in the past fifty years. What is showing up in each case is simply *selective memory*, a tendency to remember the good times while forgetting the bad. This tendency is actually a protection mechanism: it prevents our minds from being overwhelmed by the series of personal disasters which form part of any normal life. But it is a mechanism that is seriously flawed in that sometimes it can work far too well.

We have already noted Freud's discovery that thoughts and memories banished from consciousness do not disintegrate, but continue to exist at a subconscious level. In most instances, they slumber comfortably enough beneath the surface. But memories of a particularly shocking experience sometimes turn into vampires, which stir uneasily within their crypts and rise at night to drain the life-force from the individual who tried to bury them.

The soldiers in the trenches of the First World War had a particularly hard time of it. They were subjected to appalling physical conditions which sapped their vitality. (A disease known as 'trench foot' led to almost as much permanent disablement as battle injuries. It was caused by spending days, weeks and sometimes even months with your extremities in water and mud. The body literally began to rot and sometimes the only treatment was amputation.) But unlike soldiers in previous wars, they were largely denied the adrenalin highs (and exercise) of frequent pitched battles.

If all war is marked by horror, trench warfare was a particular *type* of horror, a combination of grinding boredom, gnawing fear, disease and discomfort interspersed by brief periods of pure terror. And it continued, with little respite, for years. A mind attempting to bury the worst experiences of such a period sometimes went into overload. The result was a shutdown of the systems, soldiers who behaved like zombies and became fit for nothing except hospitalization.

But shell-shock was only an extreme example of something with which psychiatrists had been familiar since Freud became interested in Breuer's patient Anna O. Anna, as we have seen, was the young woman who suffered from hysterical paralysis, sight and speech defects which were alleviated by the 'talking cure'. Although it was only vaguely suspected at the time, it now seems almost certain that Anna's condition arose out of an inability to come to terms with the death of her father. She buried his memory — and her emotional involvement with him — along with his body, but it reached out of the depths of her psyche to torment her.

Once again, the plainest pointers towards certain psychological mechanisms are drawn from the casebooks of pathology, where the grossly exaggerated nature of their appearance makes them easier to see. But it is not only (and not always) buried horrors which have influence. The way we are today is actually a summation of all our yesterdays, with our degree of emotional comfort largely dependent on how well we have assimilated previous experience. In his book *Mysteries*, Colin Wilson wrote the following incisive passage:

'If I open our family photograph album, I see a picture of me at the age of 18 months, sitting on my grandfather's shoulders. A later one shows me as an awkward looking ten-year-old, with his head on one side and a hesitant smile. If I try hard, I can remember what *that* Colin Wilson was like, because he had just been given a chemistry set and started to read science fiction. A few pages later I see myself in an RAF uniform. I can remember *him* all right. I still have a lot of the stuff he wrote. And I can remember how awkward he felt with pretty girls. By reading his work and recalling some of his embarrassments (which still make me wince) I can just about put myself inside his skin. Was he "me"? No, he certainly wasn't. Am I him? That is harder to get into mental focus; but when I succeed, I see that the answer is a qualified yes. He is a bit of me. Not too badly integrated I hope . . .

'I find myself looking at the people around me and wondering how far their various "selves" have managed to get integrated. I can think of a lot of colourless, timid people who have quite obviously fragmentary personalities. And even in a few people who seem fairly well integrated, I can suddenly catch a glimpse of a more sophisticated, confident personality that has never succeeded in emerging.'

This is a very clear, acceptable description of the way we grow from childhood to maturity in our psychic processes — if I am not the man I once was, at least the man I once was is still a part of me; and how comfortable I am with this depends entirely on how well I have managed to assimilate him.

Several years ago, following some media publicity about my investigations into reincarnation, I was approached by a woman who requested that I use her as a subject for hypnotic regression. (You will recall that the psychoanalytic term *regression* refers to the process of pushing a patient's memory back further and further in order to uncover forgotten but important incidents. In reincarnation research, the same term is used to describe a very similar process, generally involving hypnosis, which forces recall of previous lives.) I was surprised by the request. I had known the woman for some time and was aware she had neither interest nor belief in reincarnation. While I told her I would be happy to test her suitability as a regression subject, I wondered what had prompted the request. She told me she did not believe for a moment that she had lived before, but was extremely interested in the phenomenon of regression in its own right.

She was aware, of course, that the technique certainly *seemed* to produce past-life memories. Unlike myself, she did not believe these to be genuine. But she did consider them to have value, believing that the memories were spontaneous creations of the psyche and, as such, said a great deal about the unconscious of the person who created them. Her theory, in other words, was that if you produced a 'past-life' as, for example, Emily Brontë or William Shakespeare, it was clear indication of a buried desire to become a writer. If you recalled a life as a banker, it could signify an unconscious desire to have a lot of money. And so on. She was hopeful that the regression technique would persuade her own unconscious to throw up such pseudo-memories and that, by analysing the fantasies, she could learn more about her hidden hopes and fears.

This is a perfectly reasonable approach and, while I did not accept her premise, I was happy to co-operate. She regressed efficiently; the memories (or pseudo-memories) did indeed arise and she was able to see in them recognizable aspects of her waking personality. But as the experimentation continued, a new development arose. She was presented, unexpectedly, with acceptable proof that one of the 'fantasies' she created was historically accurate. After considerable research (and not inconsiderable soul-searching) she was forced to accept the literal reality of a past life.

It was a shattering experience, but also a profoundly enriching one. There is something exciting about the thought that you are the product of the various experiences throughout your life. How much more exciting then to discover you are also the product of various experiences throughout a whole daisy chain of previous lives. You are what you are, but what you are may be an Egyptian fisherman, a Nubian queen, a Roman soldier, a Victorian maid . . . If you have walked this earth before, possibly more than once, what a heady brew of previous experience now lies within your mind just waiting to be discovered. And what a fascinating web of influences combine to make you the complex personality you are today.

But if reincarnation is a fact, as you will hopefully discover for yourself before you finish with this course, its influence actually reaches *beyond* the sort of person you have come to be. For as John Donne remarked, no man is an island and you are not, of course, the only human being to have experienced the reincarnation process.

Dr Arthur Guirdham was, until his retirement, Chief Psychiatrist for the District of Bath and as sceptical about esoteric matters as only a public servant of that stature is capable of being. None the less, evidence which forced itself upon him over 44 years of medical practice, eventually convinced him not only that one of his patients had lived before, but that so too had he. More to the point, they had known one another intimately during their previous existence as Cathars in France.

As Guirdham explained in his two most important books, *The Cathars and Reincarnation* and *We Are One Another*, his investigations gradually led him to the conclusion that it was no coincidence his friend and he had met up again after a period of centuries. In their circle of acquaintances were a number of others who had also been Cathars and who had known one another 'back then'.

None of Guirdham's evidence was obtained through hypnotic regression — he derived it from sources as diverse as medical symptoms and recurring dreams — but his conclusions are borne out by a number of regression researchers, myself included. My own investigations suggest that members of the same family have often known one another before, frequently demonstrating close emotional bonds in a past life or even series of past lives.

The relationship is not always — indeed not usually — the same between one life and another. Unrelated friends in one life might be mother and son in another. Husband and wife could 'return' as brother and sister, or just good buddies. The process is complicated by the fact that sexuality is by no means fixed over a series of incarnations. The fact that you are a man in this life does not necessarily mean you were a man last time around. Some individuals seem to alternate fairly frequently between one sex and the other. Others show a statistical bias in one or other direction. It is comparatively rare to find someone who has held to the same sex consistently through every past-life investigated. This obviously complicates reincarnation relationships, since it is in the nature of human life that many close relationships are sexually based.

The *clumping* effect noted by Dr Guirdham becomes very apparent as you begin to broaden your investigations of reincarnation into your immediate circle of friends and acquaintances. It seems as if old friends really do reincarnate in groups. The reason for this is not particularly obvious, but there does seem to be something in the notion of *karmic* linkages.

The so-called *Law of Karma* is an Oriental statement roughly equivalent to the Christian doctrine that 'Whatsoever shall ye sow, so also shall ye reap' — or, in other words, you will eventually get no more than you deserve. Karma embodies both the concept of Cosmic Justice and reincarnation links. Whether the Law is accurate in its fullest expression is difficult to say, but it does seem as if there is a tendency for undischarged debts from one life to be paid off in another.

But this should not be taken too literally. The crucial factor in the linkage seems to be emotion; and the debt, whatever it may be, has to be acknowledged by both sides. There is a great deal of subtlety in the working out of these linkages and not all of them are terribly obvious. In one case from my own files, I was able to trace back the first contact between a couple who are, in this life, mother and son. Their relationship began about 2,500 years ago when the son was Captain of the Guard at a jail in which the mother was held. They became friends when he brought her news of what was happening in the outside world. Why this friendship, which was quite short-term (the jailed woman died a matter of months after their meeting), should have led to such an intimate relationship as that of mother and son is difficult to determine, although one can catch a glimmer of the mechanics.

While news of the outside world is a small enough thing in itself, it was of enormous importance to the jailed woman and may have led her to conclude her debt to the Captain was substantial. On his part, there was obviously an attraction to the woman which might, in different circumstances, have led to a much deeper friendship or even a romantic relationship. During the period of her incarceration, the Captain taught the woman, if only what was happening outside the jail. This may have established the pattern for their current relationship, since the mother would certainly have taught the son while he remained a child.

Essentially what we are looking at here are the twin factors of emotion and patterning. Together they appear to exert a major influence on the way reincarnation works.

Sometimes, of course, the emotional factors which bring people back together life after life are more clearly cut and obvious. In one case brought to my attention, two professional people, meeting for the first time, found themselves prepared to sacrifice their respective marriages (and reputations) in order to become lovers. The reason, they assured me, was that they had been lovers in a previous existence. I was not in a position to investigate the claim, so I cannot say how strong the evidence might be. But I do know from experience elsewhere that, romantic though it may sound, it is the sort of thing that *can* happen. It is not, however, inevitable. Guirdham believed a friend in this life had been his lover when they were Cathars, without either of them feeling compelled to renew the physical relationship.

Psychology, and in particular psychiatry, has taught us how certain experiences and situations can set patterns for an entire lifetime. The classic example is the sexually abused child who finds difficulties in relationships with the opposite sex forever after. But it now seems our formative years extend beyond childhood into a whole chain of childhoods, not to mention the adult experiences that followed them. The results of the influence vary from the trivial to the overwhelming. I may be nervous of the sea because I was once swept off a sailing ship and drowned. But this is of minor importance when compared to the fact that my life as a writer may be grounded in the love of words developed as a Roman scribe in Colchester.

The practical discoveries of modern psychology apply with little or no modification to the whole area of reincarnation. A psychological truism that has passed into the realms of folk wisdom is that there is no more ardent a campaigner for temperance than the reformed drunkard. But the reformation may take more than one life to come about. Peter Moss and Joe Keeton have reported on the case of the Philadelphia business executive Michael O'Mara. O'Mara today is hard-working, energetic, ambitious and abstemious. When regressed, he produced vivid recall of a life as Stephen Garrett, a Victorian layabout who was the very antithesis of all these things. Garrett lived rough in the stables and alleys of Dublin, scrounging money to spend on porter and poteen. Over a short, saturated lifetime, his mind decayed into incoherence and he died alone and penniless. Against this background, it is scarcely surprising that Michael O'Mara is what he is. His current personality seems to be structured on the determination not to go that way again.

Not all lives are so dramatic as to influence the totality of your existence next time around. The American researcher Dr Helen Wambach put it bluntly, 'Going into your past lives is like going back to your sophomore year in high school — how many times do you want to remember your gym teacher? Most past lives are pretty boring'.

The worst of ancient Chinese curses condemns you to live in 'interesting times', periods usually characterized by bloodshed, pain and similar trauma. It is interesting times which leave their psychological mark. Boring lifetimes have little far-reaching influence. But *every* lifetime has at least *some*, often in the form of a personality quirk, habit pattern or even phobia. A prime cause of the latter seems to be the act of dying.

Dr Morris Netherton, who has made a career of past-life therapy, says, 'The unresolved trauma of death is a primary cause of behavioural disorder. Most of the problems I encounter have their source in past-life deaths. When the impact of these deaths is erased, many disorders simply evaporate'. Dr Wambach echoes the same thought: 'It is quite common for my subjects to tell me that after they have experienced death in a past life, a phobia or symptom they have had has gone away'.

The findings of modern psychology make it easy for us to understand the mechanics of reincarnatory influence on our present personality and mental state. If we know that being locked in a cupboard in childhood can lead to claustrophobia, then it hardly matters whether the childhood was in this life or some other. It is far less easy to understand what mechanics lead to the repeat of *physical* illnesses from one life to another.

As you conduct your own investigations, you will have little doubt that this phenomenon really does occur — and occur in the most bizarre and intriguing ways. One of my own research subjects suffers from chronic back pain in precisely the spot where a shell ended her life when she worked as an ambulance driver in the First World War.

Dr Guirdham is quoted as saying, 'there is no disease known to man the cause of which is entirely determined in what is called his own lifetime'. And while Guirdham was a practising psychiatrist, there is little reason to believe he was referring only to psychological illness.

Dr Netherton, who pioneered reincarnation therapy in Los Angeles, first developed a real interest in the subject when he discovered he had a stomach ulcer. The problem resisted treatment until he had a vision of himself as an inmate of a Mexican institution for the criminally insane. It had the appearance of a reincarnation vision, for he somehow knew the year to be 1818. In his vision, a guard kicked him in the stomach at the spot where his ulcer appeared in his present existence. Interestingly, the memory brought immediate relief of his ulcer symptoms.

Whatever mechanics are involved in the transfer of physical trauma from one life to another, the actuality of such transfer seems to be uncommonly widespread. The American psychic Edgar Cayce, who seemed to have ready access to people's past lives while in a trance state, produced literally hundreds of readings in which the phenomenon occurred. Although not everyone takes psychics seriously, it is virtually impossible to dismiss Cayce since he managed to produce thousands of fully-documented cures based on the information he unearthed in trance — all without benefit of medical training or, indeed, much formal education.

It is all too easy to begin to view the reincarnation process as a litany of bad news — the ultimate root of many physical, emotional and mental problems. But such a view would obviously be far from accurate. Reincarnation is simply a part of the evolutionary process and as such is a mixture of good and bad, pleasure and pain. While you may look for the cause of your illnesses in past lives, you may also find your present talents began to grow there too. There seem to be two types of talent, innate and trained. But even innate talents are improved by practice; and given a modicum of determination, many talents can actually be developed in the same way. What you are today is the result of what you were *before* — and that includest the talents you exhibit and the skills you profess.

This is something which could go a long way towards explaining the phenomenon of child prodigies — themselves frequently quoted as 'proof' of reincarnation. Certain of these prodigies are extremely well known. Even those disinterested in classical music are usually vaguely aware that Mozart began composing at the age of five. But some of those less well known are even more impressive. The eighteenth century prodigie, Jean Cardiac, for example, knew the alphabet when he was three months, could converse in French at one year, in Latin at three, in English at four and in Hebrew and Greek by the time he was six. Even this record pales by comparison with Germany's famous 'infant of Lubeck', who began to talk within a few hours of his birth and went on to greater things before his premature death at the age of four.

Your own talents may be less spectacular (although hopefully your life has been a little longer) but they may be founded in part on your activities in past lives. The influence is extensive and intensely practical — and something which, as we shall see, you can turn to benefit.

Lesson Three

This one is a lot less simple than it sounds. List in your course notebook those areas of your life where you think reincarnation may have had most influence on you.

I appreciate that you do not *know* and at this stage you are not being asked to find out. What you are being asked to do is think about your life, reviewing your career, your talents, your phobias and illnesses, with special emphasis on any recurring patterns you encounter. Then note down those areas where you *suspect* reincarnation may have played a part.

Writing down your guesses is the easy part. The hard part is the self-examination that precedes it. Don't rush this: it's important. Take as much time as you need to do the job thoroughly. Once you have done this, you can then go on to the next of the exercises designed to stimulate your far memory. Try it immediately following your relaxation technique.

In this exercise, you are required to imagine yourself entering a very special kind of clothing store. It is a store which carries on its racks clothes from every country in the world. Even as you enter the store, the sheer variety of choice is bewildering, for you quickly note that not only is every country represented, but clothing from different time periods is also on display. Here is a panorama of fashion through the ages, from every culture in every clime.

As you stand bewildered, the proprietor of the store (a dapper little man in an old-fashioned frock-coat) bustles across and greets you as if you were his most honoured customer — perhaps you are, since (in the fantasy at least) you entered this store carrying an American Express gold card with unlimited credit.

'I have just the thing for you', says the proprietor and leads you through the store into a plushly carpeted private changing room at the back. On one wall is a full-length mirror. Set into another is a walk-in wardrobe. It is towards this wardrobe that the proprietor is pointing.

You walk to the wardrobe and open it. Displayed inside, is the costume the proprietor has recommended for you out of his vast selection of clothes from every country and every age. You take it out of the wardrobe, examine it closely, then put it on and study yourself in the mirror.

This done, take time to answer the following Questionnaire:

1. Describe your costume. If you know what country or time period it came from, note that down. If not, simply describe the style and material in detail. Sketch it in your notebook if you have artistic talent.

....

....

....

....

2. Make a note here of how you felt that first moment you saw the costume.

....

....

....

....

3. And how did you feel immediately after you put it on?

....

....

....

....

4. Describe how you looked while wearing the costume. Did you notice any unexplained changes in your physical appearance — hair colouring or style, build, facial characteristics etc.?

....

....

....

....

5. While you wore the costume, were you aware of any mood changes in yourself, any particular emotions, feelings or attitudes? If so, note down what they were.

....

....

....

....

6. Can you spot any linkage between the way the costume made you feel and your current attitudes and reactions? If so, list them down.

....

....

....

....

Once you have completed this exercise, go on to your next chapter. It will introduce you to a more advanced — and very dramatic — aspect of reincarnation research.

4.

Preparing for a World of Wonder

'If we could see ourselves and other objects as they really are, we should see ourselves in a world of spiritual natures.'

— Immanuel Kant

'"What is your name?"
'"Aaaaah!"
'"Are you ill?"
'"Ah . . . ah . . ."
'"Do you understand us?"
'"AHHHHH!"
'"Are you ill?"
'"AAAAAH . . . AAAAAAAAAAAH . . . Fire . . . fire . . . fire!!!"'

That disturbing little fragment is an excerpt from the regression tapes of Liverpudlian reincarnation researcher Joe Keeton, as quoted in the book *Encounters With the Past* by Keeton and Peter Moss. The hypnotized subject, a lexicographer named Sue Atkins, broke into screams of uncontrollable terror which lasted fully half a minute before she responded to commands to come out of trance. She had been reliving a past life experience in which she was lying on the floor of a burning building, unable to move, while the flames flared around her.

The reason for quoting such a dramatic extract is to ask you two straightforward questions:

How would you feel if you were Sue Atkins?

How would you feel if you were Joe Keeton?

In the course of this book, you will learn details of several techniques which will enable you to carry out reincarnation research for yourself. Among them will be the technique of hypnotic regression — the selfsame technique that sent

Sue Atkins back to the fire in the very first minutes of her very first regression.

Different subjects react to regression in slightly different ways, but many, like Mrs Atkins, do relive past life experiences. I want to be clear about this. We are not talking about remembering. We are not even talking about dreaming. We are talking about an experience so vivid *it is subjectively indistinguishable from physical reality*. When the flames lick around you, you feel the terror . . . and the pain.

Mrs Atkins was not the only one to run into trouble during a regression. *Encounters With The Past* tells of another of Keeton's subjects who, when regressed, found herself 'at the Assizes':

'"At the Assizes?" echoed Keeton. "What are you doing there? We will try to help you if we can."
'"Tis too late. 'Tis my mother, sire."
'"What about your mother, Joan?" Joe Keeton asked.
'"It is because of her I am here".
'"Of what are you accused?"
'"Witchery!!" exclaimed the subject.

It was the start of a 20-minute session marked by steadily growing tension. The trial was held at Chelmsford Assizes in 1556. Keeton's subject, a 23-year-old businesswoman was reliving the experience of an accused 17-year-old, who was stripped and pricked as part of an interrogation which left her screaming in terror, 'I know not Sathan! I know not Sathan! The child Agnes lies! She lies! Agnes lies . . .'

Both incidents are carefully selected to illustrate a vital point. Dr Wambach is perfectly right to suggest that the majority of past lives are boring, but that is not necessarily to say the majority of past life investigations follow the same pattern. With regression experiments in particular, there seems to be a tendency to gravitate towards the dramatic. I have conducted regressions in which subjects writhed in the throes of ancient fever, clung to the decks of sinking ships, died lingering deaths in lonely beds. In one, a woman was in such obvious discomfort she could scarcely speak. Afterwards she told me she had been caught in the process of having a past-life baby. Nor is the problem confined to hypnotic experiments. One of my most terrified subjects was reacting to the far memory of a fall she experienced during an experiment using the Christos Method, a technique which involves neither hypnosis nor trance.

The point about all this is that reincarnation research is not a parlour game, but a serious undertaking *with inherent dangers once you go beyond a certain stage*. I have no wish to over-emphasize the point — I would not be writing this book if I did not believe the potential gain from reincarnation research far outweighed the risks — but it is only fair to warn you clearly what you are getting into.

How dangerous then is advanced reincarnation research? What is the worst that could happen?

Although thankfully it has never happened in any experiment with which I have been involved, medical colleagues assure me the worst that could *theoretically* happen is death. Neither hypnosis, nor Christos, nor any of the other techniques commonly used are dangerous in themselves. (Indeed, the degree of relaxation possible through hypnosis is usually considered therapeutic.) But vivid, dramatic experiences such as those described earlier, could have an adverse effect on certain pre-existent physical conditions.

Plainly, if you have a serious heart condition or any other illness in which your doctor's most urgent advice is that you avoid stress, reliving a witchcraft trial or a fire is not the best possible thing you could do. Let me reiterate what I said earlier: for many people, the experience of past lives is not remembering but *reliving*. As such, the experience takes almost as much toll of the body — and just as much toll of the emotions — as did the original experience.

A good rule of thumb to remember is that if you are not fit enough to take the experience in reality, you would be well advised to keep well away from it in reincarnation research. The only trouble with this advice is that often you have no hint of what your experience will be until you are actually reliving it. At this point, the damage cannot be totally avoided, but it can be minimized. On these specific points, let me enunciate two fundamental safety rules for reincarnation research:

1. If you suffer from any physical condition in which stress is a life-threatening factor, do not permit yourself to become the subject of reincarnation research experiments *under any circumstances*.

2. Should you, for whatever reason, elect to ignore Rule 1, ensure that the experimenter conducting the research sessions is aware of your condition *and has been explicitly instructed to cut short any past life experience likely to create undue stress*.

Those are the basics. Following Rule 1 should keep you well out of trouble. Following Rule 2 could save your life if you are foolish enough to ignore Rule 1. For what it is worth, I have made it a personal rule *never* to regress any subject with a heart condition or similar illness. And even with healthy subjects, I like to have medical assistance on call wherever possible. (I have to say that simply *conducting* a regression experiment can be a stressful experience as well. Try putting yourself in the place of Joe Keeton when Sue Atkins began to scream about fire and you will see what I mean. You are a little like an Air Traffic Controller. You won't be burned in a crash, but you will certainly sweat blood to avoid one. If your doctor says your health won't stand *any* stressful situation, don't just avoid becoming a regression *subject* — avoid reincarnation experiments altogether.)

That is the worst-case scenario. If you are healthy to begin with, it will not happen. If you are not, then you can take the simple precaution of avoiding the danger. But this is not the only scenario and the next-to-worse-case, while extremely rare, is far more insidious and potentially just as lethal.

Several years ago, I was asked to conduct a regression experiment with an actress interested in reincarnation. It proved a routine enough session with the only element of note the recollection of a between-life limbo. At least, this appeared to me to be the only element of note. But something dredged up by the actress from her far memories triggered a depression, which deepened over a period of weeks until she was actively threatening suicide.

This particular case ended happily. Actual suicide was avoided and the woman eventually recovered her emotional equilibrium. But it certainly embodies a salutary lesson about reincarnation research. It is essentially the same lesson learned long ago by psychiatrists and analysts: when you begin to investigate any aspect of the human mind, you run a small, but by no means negligible, risk of probing an incipient neurosis or psychosis.

Every regression subject opens themselves up to the experience of emotional and (what certainly feels like) physical pain. As I mentioned earlier, there is a human tendency to focus on the dramatic. This tendency creates painful regressions far more often than many researchers seem prepared to admit. This is not always a bad thing. Doctors treating shell-shock eventually discovered the only real cure was to persuade their patients to remember the original trauma and relive it with a conscious discharge of all the associated emotions. But if there is a popular perception of confession, catharsis and abreaction as good for the soul, most doctors would now agree this is by no means a universal truth. There are some personalities who can only cope with trauma by ensuring it stays hidden. For such people, a forced abreaction is destructive, sometimes shattering.

The practical insights of psychology undergo little or no change when we add the knowledge of past lives to our theoretical picture. If you are unable to cope effectively with trauma in this life, you will be no different when it comes to coping with trauma in another.

Reincarnation research is, by its very nature, akin to a process of psychoanalysis. It unearths truths about yourself which have been buried deeply in your psyche for longer than you might care to remember. Some of those truths may prove therapeutic. Others may well be more than you can handle. I know of no way to avoid this latter case, except again to instruct whoever is running your experiment to cut things short if you exhibit too much stress. But even this is no absolute guarantee of safety: in the case quoted earlier, the depressive actress showed no stress whatsoever during the actual regression session.

The bottom line is simply this: you run the same emotional risks in reincarnation research as you do in psychoanalysis, without (usually) having the benefit of a trained psychiatrist to help you through them. There seems to be no foolproof way of minimizing these risks. The best you can do is be aware of them and take personal responsibility for them if they happen. That is the worst news over. But there are still elements of preparation you should undertake before embarking on full-scale research.

It has often been remarked that while there was only one historical Napoleon Bonaparte, the lunatic asylums are full of them. The same can be said, a little unkindly, but none the less with justification, for the world of reincarnation research and belief. The Victorian psychic, Daniel Dunglas Home, once remarked wittily, 'I have had the pleasure of meeting at least twelve Marie Antoinettes, six or seven

Marys of Scotland, a whole host of Louis and other kings, about 20 Great Alexanders, but never a plain John Smith. I indeed would like to cage the latter curiosity.'

Because of my interest in the subject, I have also found myself in the company of lilac people who float through life loudly claiming to have been Egyptian Pharoahs, Roman Generals, Oriental Queens or the creative great of every country. Sadly, such claims are usually based on the most flimsy of evidence or no evidence at all, and the talents of the individuals seem to have degenerated considerably since the days when they wrote the odes or routed the Goths. What is patently at work here is not reincarnation research, but wishful thinking, a desire to compensate for shortcomings in this life by claiming an impressive pedigree in one's last. It is precisely the same impulse which persuades so many people to become customers of Degree mills and vanity publishers. It is a human impulse and you would be unwise to assume you are absolutely free of it.

I would not, of course, be so impolite as to suggest you are capable of forging your past life credentials. Nor do I imagine for one moment that you would accept uncritically the first researcher who told you that you once lived as Henry VIII or Cleopatra. But I suspect you are human.

It is human to be intrigued and flattered by the possibility that you were once powerful, rich, talented or famous. It may even be that it is exactly the sort of news you most desperately need to hear in order to compensate for your perceived shortcomings in this life. In such circumstances, it is all too easy to become a little sloppy in your research, to accept the sort of evidence you might otherwise reject.

I believe the techniques of reincarnation research to be generally valid. But the parallel with psychoanalysis is close. In analysis, it is not unknown for a patient to create a fantasy, to present material which shows life not as it was, but as it might have been, perhaps should have been.

The same thing undoubtedly occurs in reincarnation research; and in many instances the fantasies are constructed with such skill and cunning that they are extremely difficult to tell apart from the real thing. This is why later in the course you will find such stress laid on research, on checking and double checking your facts. It is also why, at this stage, you should be aware of a fundamental truth: *The more flattering the pattern of a past life, the less likely it is to be true.* All apparent past-life recollections should be checked out carefully. But special care should be taken if the memories smack at all of wish-fulfilment.

Romantic past lives as known historical personalities will always fall into this category. It is not *impossible* you were once Julius Caesar, Lord Byron, Boudicca or Mrs Pankhurst, but it is frankly unlikely. Furthermore, the chances of *constructs* arising are far greater with a historical personality than an unknown, simply because the information needed to create the construct is far more readily available.

Unfortunately, the danger of self-deception does not end with known historical personalities. Without his alter ego to fall back on, the mild-mannered Clark Kent might easily construct a past life as a gladiator, warrior or explorer in order to compensate for his shortcomings in today's Metropolis. And, unless you are very wary, you might do the same.

If, as Caesar claimed, the price of peace is eternal vigilance, so too is the price of reasonable assurance that your far memories are genuine. You require a real degree of self-knowledge, a genuine realization of what makes you tick. And you need to be utterly ruthless in dismissing anything for which there is not substantial evidence . . . But not too ruthless.

The belief that one has lived before is not uncommon among celebrities. Shirley MacLaine recalls, among other past lives, that of a dancer in an Egyptian harem and a madam in the San Francisco gold rush. The pianist Liberace claimed to be a reincarnation of Franz Liszt. Yoko Ono is on record as saying that both she and John Lennon believed they had met in previous lives. Sylvester Stallone told *People* magazine he had been guillotined during the French Revolution. General George 'Blood and Guts' Patton believed he was once a Roman warrior. And, while there are a multitude of individuals who believe they were Napoleon, Napoleon himself believed he was the reincarnation of the Emperor Charlemagne. Watching a television chat-show recently, I found myself listening to a well-known actor discussing his belief that *he* had lived before. The chat-show host, who may have been a little more cynical about the subject than his guest, asked why people who remembered their past lives always remembered romantic incarnations, never dreary existences as road sweepers and lavatory attendants. I can no longer recall the answer made by the actor, but the question stuck in my mind because it is so often voiced as an objection to the validity of reincarnation research. Any serious answer to it must accept, as we have noted earlier, that the objection it embodies has more than a grain of truth in it: far too many reincarnation believers wave romantic past lives like a banner. But realistically, three things must be remembered.

The first is that the fundamental premise of the question is just plain wrong. There are quite a number of people who *do* recall past lives which were anything but glamorous. We have already noted the case of Michael O'Mara, whose greatest excitement as Stephen Garrett was where to find his next drink. Ann Dowling, another of Joe Keeton's subjects, recalled a drab life as a girl who scrubbed steps for a living. My own experience as a researcher has shown a great many subjects recall very mundane existences. The picture is sometimes confused by the appearance of a dramatic *incident* — death by fire, drowning or whatever — but a dramatic moment does not necessarily (and does not often) mean a dramatic life.

The second is that some past lives are *genuinely* dramatic and romantic, just as some present lives are dramatic and romantic. There are people today who climb Everest and fly to the moon — not many of them, but they do exist. And there have always been people who led adventurous existences. Far memory of such a life may be unusual, may be suspect, but it is not impossible.

The third, and possibly least obvious, is that distance lends enchantment — a process often mistaken for glamour. You might, for example, consider it glamorous that I had once lived as a Roman legionnaire. But would you be equally impressed were I to tell you I had just become a Private in the British Army, or a GI serving with the US Forces? I suspect not, yet all three careers are absolutely comparable. The only thing really different about the Roman army was that it was raised a little earlier in history.

Lesson Four

There is only one way I know to guard against self-deception in reincarnation research and that is to increase your level of self-awareness until you are familiar with your deepest motivations. This is, frankly, a lifetime task. But even lifetime tasks have to start somewhere . . . and this is as good a place as any.

You should by now have established your daily relaxation routine. You may even have achieved a degree of proficiency. As your task for this lesson, I would like you to build on that relaxation routine, to change it, in essence, from simple relaxation to meditation. A great deal of unnecessary mystique surrounds the practice of meditation. It does not involve trance or yoga and there is absolutely no need for you to convert to Buddhism. Indeed, like the man introduced to prose, you may even find you have been at it, unwittingly, all your life.

Starting tomorrow and continuing on a regular basis thereafter, I want you to add ten minutes or so to your morning relaxation regime. When you have totally relaxed and returned to your rhythmic 2/4 breathing, I want you to turn your attention inwards. I want you to review everything that happened to you the previous day.

This may sound a tall order if you lead a full and busy life, but the trick is not to spend too much time on any one aspect; and certainly not to begin fighting old battles or obsessing about what might have been. Simply move systematically from one part of your day to the next, carefully examining the *motives* for your actions at each point. That is actually the hard bit. As you gain proficiency, you will find that the remembering is easy. But determining your own motivations will always be a tricky job; and as you grow more skilled in the art, you will find the whole exercise becomes increasingly subtle.

The real trick is brutal honesty. Try to remember that the only person who will ever know your findings is yourself. I don't even want you to write them down in your private notebook. Furthermore, you are not trying to change anything about yourself (unless you really want to) but only to observe what it is that makes you act the way you do, think the way you do, look at things the way you do.

There are few things more fascinating than oneself. Even so, you may find your mind wandering during your meditation session. If you do, simply bring it back to the job at hand; and this time I *would* like you to jot down the problem in your notebook. Don't make a big deal of this. Your total entry to the day might read:

Meditation	Tuesday 22 February
Start	7.30 a.m.
End	7.45 a.m.
Mind-wandering......................	4
Noise interruption....................	6
Other breaks in concentration	2

The purpose of this little record is two-fold. It will remind you how often you have found some excuse to avoid meditation, as you certainly will, sooner or later. And it will provide an ongoing indicator of progress in the years ahead. As you become more proficient, you will definitely find mind-wandering and other interruptions become few and far between compared to the level they were at when you first began.

Should you find, for any reason, that you really do have to miss a moring meditation, make sure to note that in your notebook too. Here again nothing elaborate. Your entry could — and should — be something as simple as:

> *Meditation* .... Friday 6 April
>   No meditation — ill.

A few minutes non-judgemental morning meditation about your motivations can go a long way towards laying the foundations of genuine self-knowledge. Which will certainly aid you in your evaluation of reincarnation research material and may prove helpful in other aspects of your life as well.

You may even find you enjoy learning about yourself so much you are prepared to devote a few moments to the art at other times of the day — no bad thing by any criterion.

5.

The Dream Breakthrough

*'. . . the yogi is taught to enter the dream state at will . . . the practice . . .
enables its master to die and to be reborn without loss of memory — death
being the entry into a dream state and birth the awakening.'*
— W.Y. Evans-Wentz

When Pearl D. was 18 years of age, she awoke one morning to recall a fragment
of a vivid dream. In the dream, she saw herself as a young, fair-haired, white-
robed woman walking down the steps of a small but ancient amphitheatre. She
was aware of feeling faint and ill, but did not know who she was, or what she
was doing there. There the fragment ended — or at least her recall of the fragment
ended. She was intrigued by the dream, largely because it was so vivid, but could
make little sense of it and soon forgot it. Until, that is, it recurred.

Over the years, Pearl D. found herself dreaming the same dream again and
again. Not often — she might go years without its recurring — but often enough.
Over this period, a little more of the dream unfolded. In its extended version,
the dream woman reached the bottom of the steps and began to walk, with extreme
difficulty, across the arena floor. She was aware of a crowd watching her, aware
too that it was of overriding importance to reach the other side of the amphitheatre,
although she had no idea why. But whatever the reason, she did not succeed.
Half way across, her stamina gave out. She collapsed on the sand, lay for a moment
there and died.

On a very few occasions, the dream went further still. After her dream death,
Pearl D. found herself floating above her body like a wraith, looking down at
the crumpled corpse in the arena. She still did not know who she was, what
she had been doing, but oddly, all sense of urgency had vanished. Whatever she
had been trying to accomplish no longer seemed important.

Despite the death scene, it would be wrong to suggest Pearl D. found the dream disturbing. But she did find it intriguing; in particular the fact that it continued to recur over so many years. I first met her when she was in her early forties. The last instance of the dream had been only six months previously.

Pearl D. subsequently became the subject of one of the most remarkable series of regression experiments I have ever carried out. They showed conclusively that the dream was Pearl's first spontaneous eruption of far memory, the recall that sometimes bridges centuries.

It is difficult to say why this should have happened. Obviously many — indeed most — people go through life without even wondering if they have lived before, let alone remembering any of the details. But it may be that at a certain stage of personal evolution you become in some way ripe for the integration of past life material. That is to say, there may come a time when you are unable to progress without opening yourself up to the wider viewpoint reincarnation represents.

Or it may be that the reason is more routinely psychological. Incipient neuroses create pressures which send signals to the conscious mind and force it to pay attention. Since the root of such pressures can as easily be in a former life as this one, the signals may be in the form of spontaneous far memory. Whatever the reason, past life pressures do occur. Pearl D.'s case is only one among a large number on record. And nowhere is the breakthrough more likely to take place than in a dream. It is as if some part of your mind is trying to tell you that you have lived before and show you a little of what that former life was like.

Such dreams are distinctive. So distinctive, in fact, that they might be thought of as a valid tool in the investigation of your past lives. But to differentiate a reincarnation dream from the product of eating too much cheese for supper does require that you know what to look for, while to be certain of your analysis additionally requires experience and cross-checking. The dream of Pearl D. is a fairly typical experience of the genre, hence there is a good deal to be learned from it.

How then can you tell a reincarnation dream from any other? The first thing to realize is that there is no single factor which absolutely determines far memory. Virtually every pointer towards a reincarnation dream can be found, sometime, in your more mundane night adventures. You should begin to grow suspicious only when the dream you are examining shows a *collection* of such factors. The more you find, the more likely you are to be dealing with far memory.

The first thing to look for is the *reality tone* of the dream. Most dreams are milk-and-water affairs. Sleep research has shown you spend more than a third of the night dreaming (you may not *remember* but you still dream). Yet the chances are you could not even say for certain whether you usually dream in colour. The fact is, very few people pay attention to their dreams. They have a vague recollection immediately after waking, but even this fades quickly, often in less than a minute.

But sometimes a dream impinges because it is vivid. It has strong reality tone. When you awaken, you tend to remember it far longer than the average dream. The details are clear and remain clear. Strong reality tone is an indicator of far memory, or rather a *possible* indicator of far memory. Pearl D's dream was, of course, extremely vivid. When she awoke, she remembered every detail.

The next thing to look for is *lucidity*. An almost overriding characteristic of dreams is their built-in element of unreality. This is usually not apparent while you are actually dreaming. Something about the dream state encourages you to accept the most outlandish things as a matter of course. But afterwards, when you awaken, it is easy to see the dream had a melting, shifting quality. One minute you might be in London, the next in New York, and all without benefit of aeroplane or other means of transport.

If you are prepared to leave aside the closing moments when she looked down on her body, there were no fantasy elements in the arena dream of Pearl D. Time flowed sequentially. Things remained as they were, refusing to change into something else. With the sole exception of those final moments, she might have been experiencing reality — and we may even have something to say later about those final moments. The next question you should ask yourself is *did the dream recur*? The arena dream did, of course — it was this factor more than any other which intrigued Pearl D. As, undoubtedly, it was meant to.

Reincarnation dreams arise out of a pressure condition in the depths of the psyche. They are an attempt to attract the attention of the conscious mind, to suggest, in effect, that perhaps the time has come for you to begin thinking a little further than the here and now. But very few of us pay attention immediately. Or, if we do, very few of us understand at once what the dream is all about. Thus it repeats and will continue to repeat until the message gets through. Although Pearl D. endured and ejoyed her arena dream throughout the whole of her adult life, it stopped with her first experience of conscious regression and has not recurred since. Her personal awareness of the reincarnation process relieved the pressure.

Vivid dreams . . . lucid dreams . . . recurring dreams . . . In isolation, each of these aspects means little. But find all three together and you may begin to suspect the action of far memory. There are, however, a number of other factors you should look for before allowing that suspicion to grow.

One is how you *see yourself* in the dream. In most dreams you function as you function in your waking life, from the *inside*. You look out on the world from behind your eyes; events take place around you. In some dreams, however, you see yourself as if you were seated in a theatre, watching a movie or a play. One of the characters portrays you on the stage, but the essential you is somewhere outside, an observer. The situation is quite distinctive and represents another characteristic of far memory, although usually only if taken in tandem with another, associated characteristic.

Given that you can *see yourself* in a dream, that you can watch yourself operate out there like an actor or actress, it is necessary to ask yourself whether you look as you look now. If you have brown hair, is your hair still brown in the dream? If you are of slim build, are you still of slim build in the dream? What you are really asking is whether the dream you is the same you as the familiar you of waking life.

We need to be careful here. Very few of us see ourselves as we really are. Body image, your personal perception of your physical build, sometimes diverges considerably from the reality. But if the starving anorexic still manages to see herself as fat, the distortion of her perceptions does not usually extend to imagining her eyes are blue when they are actually brown. When you analyse your dream for far memory, you are not searching for differences in the way you perceive yourself. You are looking for a dream in which you are a wholly different person.

One of the most interesting things about Pearl D.'s dream was that its central character did not change as Pearl herself got older. The dream first appeared when Pearl was about 18. The woman in the dream, who did not look at all like Pearl in reality, was perhaps a few years older, in her early twenties.

But as Pearl passed through her own twenties, then thirties, then arrived at her forties, the dream character did not age at all. It was as if Pearl was watching the return of a movie made about a specific incident in her life (as it transpired she was . . . in a sense.)

Hot on the heels of how your dream self may look comes the question of how your dream self *behaves*. This one is a great deal more difficult to analyse than simple physical appearance. There is no doubt at all that many normal dreams (i.e. dreams which have no element of far memory) frequently contain instances of *compensation*. If you are a timid character in real life, you may dream you are engaged on heroic deeds; and few men can honestly claim never to have dreamed of making love to women other than their wives.

But compensatory mechanisms aside, there are dreams in which you still behave out of character, and in ways which seem to defy easy explanation. Your dream self seems to have picked up habits or quirks which are not apparent in your waking life. In the dream, your usual priorities or interests may have changed. Subtle changes of this type are always worth exploring if you are hunting for far memory.

But the emphasis is very much on that word *subtle*. The dominant characteristics of dream self and real self are often identical. In the arena dream, for example, the dominant characteristic of its central player was dogged determination. She knew she had to cross the amphitheatre and pushed herself to do so, literally to the point of death. The same sort of determination is very obvious as a central trait in the waking Pearl D.

Where differences tend to arise is the area of *mores* — those patterns of behaviour that are *culturally conditioned*. An example might be the elaborate, hat-sweeping bow affected by French noblemen of the seventeenth century. Such a custom appears overdone to us now, even in France, so that its appearance in a dream might well be taken as uncharacteristic behaviour.

With so much emphasis placed on differences, it may be as well to note that however different the central character of a reincarnation dream may look or behave, you will have no doubts about that character's identity. There is something in you that reaches down the years with instant recognition of what you once were.

So far, we have touched on the broader pointers towards the reincarnation dream. Now it is time to consider a few specifics. These might begin with how you were dressed in the dream. What you are obviously looking for is a style of dress which indicates a different age. It is a long time since three-cornered hats were in fashion and if you find yourself sporting a toga, you might reasonably conclude something a little odd was going on. In the arena dream, Pearl D. found herself dressed in a white robe vaguely reminiscent of Ancient Greece and certainly a far cry from anything she would be likely to wear today. But sometimes, like many another reincarnation clue, the differences can be subtle. Check your footwear and the *details* of your clothing. Something as small as a brooch, a ring or a cravat may be as much as you will find.

Let's summarize again. Vivid dreams . . . lucid dreams . . . recurring dreams . . . how you see yourself . . . how you look . . . how you behave . . . what you are wearing . . . All this before you even consider what might seem the most obvious factor of all: the *environment* of the dream.

In Pearl D.'s dream, the environment was very obviously archaic. She was in an amphitheatre. The crowd on the terraces were dressed in robes and tunics. A Mediterranean sun shone brightly out of a cloudless sky. Outside of a film set, such an environment would be difficult to find today. But it is characteristic of much of the Classical ancient world.

Finally, your attention should focus on *content*. What was *happening* in the dream? What was the main *concern* of the central character? In the arena dream, Pearl D.'s main concern remained a mystery which went unresolved until she undertook regression. But there were other details that were intriguing. One was that the arena crowd shouted encouragement. She was obviously a highly popular figure.

It may seem I am stressing the obvious in all this. There is a definite temptation to view Pearl D.'s arena dream with hindsight and assume any fool could see it had to do with reincarnation. But this really will not do — not for the arena dream and not for any similarly suspicious dreams you may someday require to analyse. Because once you have determined there are sufficient indicators to suggest a dream *might* be a manifestation of far memory, you have to ask yourself what else it might be.

Despite a great deal of research, no one is certain of what precise part dreams play in the human psyche. There seems to be little doubt they are important: if you are deprived of your dreams for a time, you will eventually engage in an orgy of dreaming to catch up. But the essential nature of their importance eludes us. We do know, however, that some dreams carry (often symbolic) messages from one level of our mind to another and that some dreams reflect our waking interests and concerns. It is that latter point which turns reincarnation dream research into a minefield.

If you were, for example, a professional soccer player, it might seem odd should you begin to dream of Victorian London. But if you were a history professor specializing in nineteenth century social conditions, no one would think it odd at all. Unfortunately, life is nowhere nearly so simple as this example pretends. There is no reason why the soccer player should not have an interest in Victoriana. For all we know, his favourite author may be Dickens and his home full of nineteenth century antiques. Against such a background, the soccer player's dream no longer appears very unusual either.

The problems do not stop there. Even if you have *no* overriding interest in the reign of Queen Victoria, it is possible you watched a period movie on television before retiring to bed? Or within the past week? Or saw something or heard something which triggered associations with such a movie? Or have you, perhaps, just finished a book on the subject — John Fowles' brilliant best-seller *The French Lieutenant's Woman* perhaps? And if not a book, were you leafing through a magazine article on Victorian architecture? Or a newspaper report which mentioned Jack the Ripper?

You can begin to appreciate the problems. Reincarnation research is not just a question of having a peculiar dream. You need to hunt diligently for the *root* of that dream; and you are entitled to postulate far memory only if you are unable to find it in a more obvious place.

Pearl D.'s dream was suggestive, but by no means conclusive. It had, however, two additional elements which, if hardly typical of far memory dreams, at least give you an indication of the type of thing you might begin to look for.

The first element was the amphitheatre itself. When one hears of an ancient arena, the mind tends to jump to the gladiatorial carnage of Ancient Rome or the less messy dramas of Classical Greece. But Pearl D., who was as familiar with Greek and Roman ruins as any educated and well-travelled individual, found her dream amphitheatre like neither. It seemed to be too small, for one thing; and the architecture was wrong. Indeed, the architectural style was totally unfamiliar to her.

This is interesting, for if the arena were a construct, a fantasy created for its own amusement by her unconscious mind, one might imagine familiar materials would be used to built it — that is to say, she would have used a Greek or Roman model.

The second element was the behaviour of the crowd. Typically, the Roman mob howled for blood. Spectators at Greek plays were appreciative or critical, depending on the skill of the performance. But the audience in Pearl D.'s theatre did not fit either picture. They were extremely quiet for the most part, intensely interested and, she felt, supportive. If she were to be thrown to the lions, it was obvious no one in the crowd approved . . . but then, of course, there was nothing in her dream to suggest she *was* being thrown to the lions.

As it later transpired, Pearl D.'s arena dream really was an example of far memory. Something in the depths of her mind reached out to remind her she had once lived in a country whose boundaries appear on no modern map. The dream was vivid, dramatic and recurrent, because, one assumes, that something felt it important to attract Pearl's waking attention. But not all far memory in dreams presents itself in quite so spectacular a manner. You have a wellspring of past-life recollection slumbering in your psyche. Such memories are not always under pressure, as Pearl D.'s obviously were. But there can be something a little like a *leakage*.

If you forget about reincarnation dreams for a moment and concentrate on the more typical overnight adventure, you will find your dreams are composed of a number of different elements, some presented in distorted or symbolic form. It seems as if you take incidents from life and combine them in a shifting panorama of images played out before your sleeping mind. In his famous *Experiment With Time*, Dunne quoted a brief case study which demonstrates graphically how real-life incidents are changed then incorporated into our dreams. In the dream, the sleeper had a vision of people throwing lighted cigarettes towards him. None struck him or burned him, but flashed past his face in a steady stream. In the waking incident which triggered the dream, the man was cutting a plank of wood with a circular saw. The saw struck a nail in the plank and a stream of sparks flew out towards his face.

Dunne argued that the waking trigger for many dream elements might be as easily drawn from *future* experience as from the past. Whatever one thinks about this intriguing theory, there is some evidence to suggest the occasional trigger may be drawn from a past life. Such triggers are a lot less easy to spot than the sort of full-blown reincarnation dream we have been considering. They require you to sift through dream material for extremely subtle clues. You might, for example, find that in a dream about present-day New York, you are wearing Egyptian earrings in the style of the Second Dynasty. Or the hint might be more subtle still — a word in an unknown language . . . a flash of an unfamiliar scene . . . the brief appearance of an archaic character . . . an anachronistic incident . . . and so on.

This style of research is difficult, specialized, and usually extremely frustrating when compared to an investigation of the more spectacular reincarnation dream like that of Pearl D. But it has one great advantage in that it is more controllable. The drawback with the full-blown reincarnation dream is that you can do nothing at all to stimulate it: such dreams simply happen. You could wait a lifetime to have one; and even then you might be waiting forever. But you can investigate *any* dream for hints of far memory leakage. And as we have already noted, you dream every night.

Lesson Five

The famous recipe for rabbit stew begins, 'First catch your rabbit . . .' Dream research is a little like that. Your first big problem is to catch your dream.

Of course, if you are prey to the sort of spectacular recurring dream that came to Pearl D., you will have no problem at all. Such dreams force themselves on consciousness and continue to make a fuss, often over many years, until you begin to take them seriously. But the chances are you will have very few such dreams to work on. Consequently you will have to sift through more routine dream material with all the care, attention and patience of a prospector panning for gold.

The techniques of analysis already discussed in relation to the full-blown reincarnation dream are all valid for this type of prospecting. The only difference is the richness of the vein on which you are working. But before you can apply them to the dreams you will have tonight, you are going to have to learn one more technique — the one that lets you catch the rabbit.

Everybody dreams, but almost nobody *remembers*. The alarm clock wakes you in the morning with your head full of colour and action and by the time you get out of bed, it is all gone, evaporating like morning mist under a summer sun. The technique of remembering is simple to describe, but requires a truly enormous act of will to carry through. None the less, I hope you *will* carry it through, for apart altogether from reincarnation research it opens up a whole fresh area of interest and experience which has, most certainly, been largely lost to you for years.

When you go to bed tonight — and every night thereafter — I want you to equip yourself with a special notebook and pen or pencil. Leave them beside your bed, on a table or on the floor, but close enough so you can reach them easily without having to get out of bed to do so. The notebook is your dream notebook. When you awake from sleep, in the middle of the night or tomorrow morning, I want you to make a note of any dream memories you may have. The trick is to do it at once. If you wait for even half a minute, the dream will have begun to crumble round the edges. If you wait to get out of bed, it will have gone completely.

This may sound easy enough now, but when you are warm in bed, relaxed and sleepy, it will become the most difficult thing in the world. None the less I want you to try, and to keep on trying. Learn to write in the dark. Develop the technique of noting down salient points to jog your memory. The good news is that the more often you force yourself to do this, the easier it will become. Eventually, noting down your dreams will become a habit, at which point you will wonder why you ever thought it difficult. (Some people find it easier to describe their dreams into a small tape recorder left beside the bed. If this method works better for you, use it — although it can cause problems for those who share beds with a sleeping partner.)

Having captured your dreams in whichever form, write them up in detail in the same book in which you keep the record of your daily meditation. When you have written them up, apply the techniques we have discussed in order to sift out any elements which seem to you suggestive of far memory. Make a note of these alongside the dream itself.

It is a rare thing for dream analysis to present you with conclusive *proof* of a past life (although Dr Guirdham sifted some interesting evidence out of patients' dreams) but, as you become skilled, you may be pleasantly surprised to discover how many interesting and intriguing *pointers* you find.

What you are doing, of course, is creating a comprehensive record of your inner life, one which should contain at least some far memory elements. Such elements are extremely useful in guiding you towards further areas of research and may themselves become part of a wider research pattern which might include one or more of the more advanced techniques discussed later in this course.

Take at least a week to practise dream capture and analysis before moving on to your next lesson.

6.

The Practice of Hypnosis

'Freud discovered that under (hypnotic) influence patients were sometimes able to remember and disclose emotions and experiences of which they had no knowledge in consciousness.'

— David Stafford-Clark

In 1905, Carl Jung became lecturer in psychiatry at the University of Zurich, a position he held until 1913. During his first semesters, his lectures dealt chiefly with the work of Janet and Flournoy . . . and with hypnosis. The latter lectures were often enlivened by practical demonstrations. One such demonstration involved a 58-year-old woman who arrived on crutches, led by her maid. For 17 years she had suffered from a painful paralysis of her left leg.

Jung invited her to sit in a comfortable chair then, as was his custom, asked her to relate a little of her personal history to give an audience of 20 students the context of her illness. She proved only too willing and launched into a tale of woe so detailed and prolonged that it threatened to fill the entire lecture period. Eventually, however, Jung interrupted her to say, 'Well now, we have no more time for so much talk. I am now going to hypnotize you'. At which point the woman closed her eyes and fell into a profound trance *with no hypnotic induction whatsoever.*

Jung was taken aback at this, but said nothing. Indeed he had little opportunity to say anything since the woman continued to talk without pause. Now she no longer spoke about her illness, but about her dreams. Jung, growing increasingly uncomfortable, concluded she had fallen into some sort of mysterious delirium. (In later years, he decided it was nothing of the sort, but that the dream she related represented a fairly deep experience of the unconscious. At the time, however, he was still too inexperienced to make this interpretation.)

The woman talked for half an hour, after which Jung felt he should make some move to awaken her. He issued the appropriate commands . . . and nothing happened. He issued them again and still nothing happened. Thoroughly alarmed by now, he began to wonder if he had inadvertently probed some latent psychosis. Still the woman droned on and on. For ten minutes, desperately hiding his discomfort from his students, Jung tried to waken her. When she finally regained normal consciousness she was giddy and confused. 'I am the doctor and everything is all right,' Jung told her firmly. At which point she called out, 'But I am cured!' She stood up, threw away her crutches and proceeded to demonstrate that she could walk.

A flushed Jung turned to his student audience and remarked, 'Now you have seen what can be done with hypnosis!' In fact, as he admitted in his autobiography *Memories, Dreams, Reflections*, he had not the least idea what had happened and the incident became one of the reasons why he abandoned hypnosis in his clinical practice.

Many hypnotists would, I think, feel considerable sympathy for Jung in this amusing little anecdote. While the techniques of hypnosis have been known and used for millenia — it seems to have been practised in Ancient Greece and Egypt and, even earlier, in Ancient India — any genuine understanding of the phenomenon remains elusive. The most experienced practitioners are, like Jung, sometimes taken aback by what happens and at a loss to find an explanation for it.

Even our modern term for the art, *hypnosis*, is in error. It derives from the Greek *hypnos*, meaning 'sleep'. But there is no relationship at all between hypnotic trance and sleep, despite the superficial similarities that persuaded James Braid to coin the term.

An older, far more descriptive, term for hypnosis is *mekhenesis*, which means 'the taking away of responsibility'. And if this does not tell us how or why hypnosis works, it does at least pinpoint one of the most important characteristics of the trance state. When you place someone under hypnosis, you take away their responsibility for what happens. As the hypnotist, you are in control — and the control is total.

This is a disturbing situation which has created its own mythology. No one likes to imagine his free will is so fragile that another might break it completely. Hence it is often alleged that hypnotized subjects can never be made to do anything that runs contrary to their moral principles. To support the assertion, another amusing anecdote from the early days of psychiatry is often quoted.

According to this story, Charcot was demonstrating hypnosis to a group of male students. In contrast to Jung's garrilous middle-aged lady, Charcot's subject was an extremely attractive young woman. Charcot had placed her in trance when a message arrived calling him away to attend to some urgent business. He passed control of the subject to an assistant and left the lecture hall. The young man who was now in charge did not, however, exhibit that sobriety of purpose for which medical students are generally noted. Instead, to the delight of his audience, he commanded the young woman to remove all her clothes. Her eyes flicked open, she emerged at once from trance and slapped his face.

While the story has always struck me as Freudian in more ways than one, I have no doubt that something like it may actually have happened; or, if not, certainly *could* have happened. In his *Sense and Nonsense in Psychology*, Professor

H.J. Eysenck remarks that, 'There are many observations of this kind to be found in the experimental literature and it may be said with a reasonable degree of confidence that in many cases an *explicit suggestion to do something unethical or immoral will not be carried out by the subject'* (his italics).

But the critical word here is *explicit*. Experimental research has shown conclusively that with a little imagination, a deeply hypnotized subject can be made to do just about anything you want him, or her, to do.

Some of the experimentation produced disturbing results. Professor Eysenck quotes the case of a serving soldier who was persuaded to desert by means of post-hypnotic suggestion. This means that he was placed in trance and given instructions which he would carry out, on a given signal, *after* he regained normal consciousness. Typically, subjects reacting to post-hypnotic suggestion have no conscious awareness they are doing so and consider themselves to be acting under their own volition. Often they will create elaborate rationalizations to explain their behaviour.

Even in peacetime, desertion is a court-martial offence and the soldier in question would have faced severe disciplinary action had the circumstances of the experiment not been known. But more to the point, the offence runs contrary to the most fundamental military conditioning. There is no reason to assume the subject here was anything other than a model soldier. Desertion must have gone against everything he believed about the way a soldier should conduct himself.

Post-hypnotic suggestions are subtle. They creep under your normal defences precisely because you are seldom consciously aware you have recieved one. But a straightforward command while the subject is in trance — even one as crass as that delivered by Charcot's assistant — *will* be obeyed, *provided* it is properly framed. Another army experiment bears this out.

The subject of the second experiment was a 20-year-old Private with an excellent Army record. He was hypnotized while several senior personnel looked on. One of them, a Lieutenant-Colonel, was placed directly in front of him, about ten feet away. It was then suggested to the subject that when he opened his eyes he would see 'a dirty Jap soldier'. This soldier, he was told, had a bayonet in his hand and murder in his heart. The subject was urged to 'strangle him with your bare hands'.

In a moment the subject opened his eyes and began very slowly to move forward. Then he launched himself in a flying tackle and brought the Lieutenant-Colonel crashing to the floor. He then knocked the officer against the wall and tried to strangle him. Three people were required to pull him off and he was only finally pacified when the experimenter placed him in trance again. The officer who was subject to the attack confirmed that there was nothing make-believe about it and considered he would have been seriously injured had assistance not been immediately available. But would he?

The most serious objection to this experiment is that the conditions under which it was carried out precluded a definitive result. Attacking a senior officer is, of course, almost as serious a military offence as desertion. But the soldier in this instance *knew* he was taking part in an experiment, *knew* he was being ordered by the hypnotist to do something he would not normally do. And, above all, *knew* all this was taking place with the full knowledge and consent of the military authorities.

In other words, the circumstances were such that they created a wholly unreal situation. The soldier might have concluded he could attack the Lieutenant-Colonel and get away with it . . . as indeed he did. What we are left with is an experiment that is suggestive, but little more. And Professor Eysenck's description leaves us in some doubt about whether the soldier was acting under hypnotic or post-hypnotic suggestion.

But no such objections can be levelled at the most disturbing experiment of all, carried out in the early 1950s. Here subjects were shown the destructive power of nitric acid when a penny was thrown into a bowl of the liquid and disintegrated. They were then placed in trance and instructed to throw the acid into the face of an assistant. For obvious reasons, a substitute was made for the actual acid. While the subject was distracted, the experimenters put in its place a similar bowl of water to which methylene blue and barium peroxide had been added. The mixture resulted in an impressively boiling liquid indistinguishable from the real thing.

Predictably, direct orders to throw the acid resulted in the same sort of rejection suffered by Charcot's assistant. But the experimenters quickly discovered they could persuade subjects to accept a variety of fantasies in which they were all too willing to take violent action. One entranced woman was, for example, told that the assistant was a murderer who was coming to kill her child.

At face value, there is still room for objections. We might wonder, for instance, how adroitly the safe bowl was substituted for the actual acid. Any suspicion by the subject that the liquid was harmless would, of course, invalidate the whole experiment. Fortunately for the march of science what was charmingly described as 'a most regrettable mistake in technique' occurred during the experimental series. Someone forgot to switch the bowls; and the hypnotized subject did not hesitate to throw the (real) acid.

There is a lesson in all this. Hypnosis is one of the most powerful reincarnation research tools yet developed. You will use it yourself as you continue this course, either by developing your own abilities as a hypnotist or presenting yourself as a regression subject. In the latter case, the lesson of the foregoing experiments is clear: *Make sure you can trust your hypnotist.*

In point of fact, not every hypnotic subject is capable of being regressed. Individual reactions to induction techniques vary enormously. One measure of this variation is something called the Eysenck-Furneaux Scale, based on how often a particular suggestion was accepted within a large group of hypnotic subjects. The scale runs from simple fundamental suggestions like those of tired eyes or complete relaxation, which are accepted in 76 per cent of cases, all the way through to suggestions which create the illusion of an electric bulb lighting up, something successfully achieved in only 12 per cent of cases. That 12 per cent is interesting, since it coincides roughly with the frequently quoted statistic that about 10 per cent of the population are capable of achieving a deep trance state. The term *deep trance* arises out of another, five-fold, categorization of hypnotic phenomena as follows:

Category 1: Insusceptible

Here subjects show a total lack of response to suggestion. This is not to say they are *fighting off* the suggestions — they may be perfectly willing, indeed anxious, to be hypnotized, but the technique simply does not work at any level.

Categrory 2: Hypnoidal

This category is characterized by relaxation, some fluttering of the eyelids usually followed by actual closing of the eyes. Subjectively the body feels heavy.

Category 3: Light Trance

When this level is achieved, it becomes virtually impossible for subjects to open their eyes or move their limbs without specific instructions to do so. Suggestions of rigidity are readily accepted and it is possible to induce what is technically termed 'glove anaesthesia'. Glove anaesthesia arises when, on command, no pain can be felt in the hands — the area covered by a glove.

Category 4: Medium Trance

At this level spontaneous amnesia arises — a partial or total inability to remember what happened during trance. Subjects may be persuaded to undergo temporary personality changes and will react to simple post-hypnotic suggestions, including post-hypnotic anaesthesia.

Category 5: Deep Trance

Deep trance is characterized by the subjects' ability to open their eyes without affecting the trance, the acceptance of bizarre and complex post-hypnotic suggestions, including post-hypnotic hallucination, auditory hallucinations and selective directed post-hypnotic amnesia. In deep trance, hallucinations may be negative as well as positive: that is to say you can be persuaded to hear nothing when someone speaks to you as readily as you can be persuaded to hear voices when none are present. Directed amnesia arises when you obey commands to forget specific experiences during trance, but not others.

Although some instances of past-life recall have been achieved at the medium level, deep trance is required if you are to pursue your experiments with any real confidence of success. This naturally leads to the question of how often deep trance can be achieved. And the first thing you will discover is that the accepted 10 per cent figure mentioned earlier is in error.

Statistical analysis caused Professor Eysenck to suggest that about 15 per cent of the population are insusceptible, 40 per cent can achieve either light trance or the hypnoidal state, 25 per cent reach medium trance and 20 per cent are capable of going all the way to deep trance.

These figures do not tally particularly well with the Eysenck-Furneaux Scale which, for example, shows only a 15 per cent instance of spontaneous amnesia, a characteristic of medium level trance, hence something one would expect to find in 25 per cent of cases. Nor, for what it is worth, do they tally all that well with my own experience.

At the low end of the scale, I have only ever found two *completely* insusceptible subjects — father and son — in more than three decades of hypnotic practice. At the high end, while I have made no formal statistical analysis, my impression is that the number of people capable of achieving deep trance is much nearer one-in-three than the quoted one-in-five.

It may not be all that difficult to explain the discrepancies. There is nothing mechanical about hypnosis. It arises out of an interaction between two human beings and, as such, is only as susceptible to statistical analysis as, for example, musical talent. A subject one hypnotist finds impossible to put under may achieve deep trance with another. Or with the same hypnotist at a different time. One of my most amenable deep trance subjects was like that. I tried for several weeks to hypnotise him with no success whatsoever; and only managed the trick (without quite knowing how) when he asked me to make one last attempt after watching me work with another subject.

There may be a question of motivation here. Whatever the statistics may suggest, hypnotic studies are not carried out on the public at large. Those who present themselves to a hypnotist usually have some motive for doing so. They may wish to stop smoking, achieve a better degree of relaxation, increase self-confidence or whatever. Even in stage demonstrations, there is considerable pre-selection and results are always modified by factors like exhibitionism. Against this background, we can see a subject is not merely motivated to *visit* the hypnotist, but also to achieve an acceptable level of trance. I have yet to see proof that these are factors which would influence statistical results in specific cases, but I strongly suspect they might be.

Within the overall phenomenon of hypnosis, the reality of regression is well established, as is its validity, at least when regression is defined in a strictly psychological manner and does not include the concept of past lives. Even Professor Eysenck, who considers claims of intra-uterine memories to be 'absurd' (and presumably regards reincarnation recall even less favourably) wholly accepts the remarkable memory improvement possible through hypnosis and is impressed by the evidence presented by regression subjects. Such evidence is, in fact, extremely interesting. Although it does not relate directly to reincarnation research, it certainly does tend to validate one of the most important reincarnation research tools.

When regressed to an early age, the subject will typically adopt the limited vocabulary of that age and may even begin to speak in a childlike tone. Personality changes occur. Behaviour patterns become those of the suggested age level. If a drawing is requested, it shows a childlike technique. Most interesting of all are the handwriting changes, which often conform precisely to handwriting samples produced by the subject when he was *actually* of the age suggested.

In one experiment, a 20-year-old woman regressed by stages, switched the chalk to her left hand when it was suggested she was six years old. She was, it transpired, born left-handed, but forced to switch to her right hand once she entered the educational system. The phenomenon of changed handedness has been seen quite frequently in regression experiments; and has arisen spontaneously in cases where the subject had no conscious memory of ever being left-handed. In such cases, parents or older relatives would usually confirm the regression results. If the question of handedness strongly suggests regression subjects are not simply acting out an appropriate part, a whole series of other experiments proves it conclusively.

The most spectacular of these involved a 30-year-old male subject who was seated in a special chair psychologists use to stimulate emotional reaction. (It has a catch which causes it to fall backwards abruptly into a horizontal position.) When regressed to the age of one year, the chair was triggered and the man flung back. As an adult, he would have been expected to extend his arms and legs in a reflex compensatory action. In his regressed state, he screamed, fell back, and urinated in his trousers.

Examination of eye movements indicates that when subjects are regressed to an early age, their ocular coordination degenerates. In two specific cases, opthalmic examination produced even more impressive results. With one subject, who had worn glasses since the age of 12, regression to the age of seven produced a measurable improvement in vision — a development most opticians would insist was quite impossible to create clinically. The second subject had actually suffered blindness in the left half of the right eye, due to the presence of a colloid cyst in the third ventricle. When the cyst was surgically removed, his sight returned to normal. But when regressed to a time before the operation, the visual defect reappeared.

There is, in fact, an interesting test you can try out for yourself, providing you do not alert the subject to what is expected. If you stroke the sole of an adult foot, a neurophysiological response known as the Babinski Reflex causes the big toe to turn downwards. if a subject is effectively regressed to infancy prior to the age of seven months and the sole stroked, a reversed reaction should occur — the big toe turning *upwards* as it does in all babies.

In the next chapter, which deals specifically with the actual technique of regression, I shall be giving you an even more certain test that the procedure is working effectively. But for the moment, the only point being made is that the process of hypnotic regression is not an 'as if' phenomenon. Test after test has shown that subjects *relive* earlier periods of their life in a physiological as well as psychological manner. The response to a reincarnation regression is no different. A novel, vivid and potentially important experience is usually produced, with physiological as well as psychological elements.

The tool which produces these fascinating experiences is hypnosis. And in the practical section of this lesson, it is a tool you will, hopefully, learn to use.

Lesson Six

Perhaps the most novel technique for inducing hypnosis arose when a London psychologist, who had spent many hours in a vain attempt to produce even an hypnoidal response, finally lost his temper and shouted at his subject, 'Oh go to sleep, you silly sod!' At which point the subject closed his eyes and passed into a profound trance.

There are many other ways of doing it, all of them effective, most of them at least a little less bizarre than the example quoted above. The method I plan to teach you here is simple, direct, logical and has the distinct benefit that you know most of it already.

Have your subject sit comfortably or, better still, lie down on a couch or bed. If necessary, take a little time to discuss the nature of hypnosis and allow him to voice any fears he may have about it. Do all you can to reassure him that there is no danger associated with the trance state (which there isn't) and that there will be no problem in waking him up afterwards. (The question of waking up worries inexperienced subjects far more than hypnotists, who know the real difficulty is getting into trance, not getting out again. Despite Jung's embarrassing experience, very few subjects show the slightest resistance to wake-up commands. Perhaps more reassuring still is the result of an experiment of my own. My subject, a physicist, was curious to know what would happen if *no* command was given to come out of trance. With his agreement, I hypnotized him, tested the trance level — which was reassuringly deep — then simply left him. He emerged spontaneously from trance after about 15 minutes.)

When your subject is reassured, invite him to make himself comfortable — suggest he loosens his tie, removes his shoes or does whatever else he needs in order to relax. Explain that you require his cooperation during the induction process, that no one can be hypnotized against his will. (This is actually quite true, although only for first-time subjects. Once deep trance has been successfully induced, a subject can be triggered to reproduce the state on command — a type of post-hypnotic suggestion that is notoriously difficult to fight off.) Tell him hypnosis is largely a matter of progressive relaxation and that you are about to show him a method by means of which he can achieve substantial tension release. Then direct him through exactly the relaxation sequence you practise each morning before your meditation.

If necessary — and it sometimes is with nervous subjects — you can run him through the entire sequence more than once. The aim is to encourage as high a degree of physical relaxation as possible. Once you are satisfied your subject is as relaxed as he is going to get, proceed with the actual induction.

The technique you are going to use involves 'stacking' increasingly complex suggestions until a satisfactory trance level is achieved. It is based on the discovery that a subject persuaded to accept one suggestion is more likely to accept another;

and that the second suggestion may be structured to push things a little further than the first. What evolves from this is a gradual process by means of which the subject is slowly led further and further from normal consciousness, one small step at a time.

Begin the process by asking your subject to open his eyes (if he has closed them) and fix his gaze at a spot *above* eye level. You can, if you wish, hold something for him to look at (the cartoon picture of the steely-eyed Svenghali dangling a watch is not *all* fiction) but a crack in the ceiling or a picture on the wall will do just as well. The important thing is that he is forced to look upwards. This creates a physiological reaction which causes the eyes to tire quite quickly. Begin the hypnotic induction by telling him quietly, firmly and repeatedly that his eyes are growing tired.

You can see straight away what is happening here. You have set up a situation in which your subject's eyes tire rapidly while at the same time suggesting his eyes are tired. Your subject naturally accepts the initial suggestion because it happens to be true: his eyes really are getting tired. But it is unlikely that he will understand there is a perfectly good physical explanation for it. At some level he is far more likely to assume the tiredness is due to your hypnotic induction technique. In other words, he will see himself as having accepted your first suggestion; and having done so, will be all the more likely to accept your second.

Your second suggestion builds on the first. You should tell him, quietly, firmly, repeatedly, that his eyelids are growing heavy. Like your first suggestion, this one is something of a cheat. Once your eyes begin to tire, your body will start to issue increasingly urgent demands that you rest them. But your subject is being required to continue in the situation which produced the tiredness. He is still looking upwards, his vision focused on a specific point. He cannot ease the tiredness as he normally would simply by looking at something else. Thus his body will seek to persuade him to *close his eyes*. But he cannot immediately do this either (because you have instructed him to keep his eyes open). A minor, but very real, conflict arises. His eyelids will begin to droop, then snap open. Your first indication of success in your technique will almost certainly be the flickering of the eyelids which arises out of this conflict.

Throughout, you are, of course, continuing to insist that his eyelids are growing heavy — which is, of course, exactly what he is feeling. Another suggestion has been accepted and your subject is consequently more predisposed to accept the next.

Once you spot the distinctive flicker, you can resolve your subject's conflict by suggesting that his eyelids are now so heavy he can no longer hold them open, that his eyes are slowly sinking shut. This suggestion is often accepted at once, or very quickly. The eyelids close.

What you have on your hands at this point is a reasonably amenable subject, one who has begun the process of accepting suggestions. Remind him that you require his co-operation and ask him to concentrate on his breathing so that he establishes a deep, even rhythm. Do *not* attempt to establish 2/4 breathing: the technique is too distracting for a beginner.

Monitor the process of the subject's breathing as you continue to deliver suggestions in a low, firm, confident tone. When an easy rhythm is established, begin to suggest he is experiencing the sensation of total relaxation. This suggestion is given a high 76 point rating on the Eysenck-Furneaux scale, but you have actually increased its acceptability by taking him through a physical relaxation process to begin with. He should certainly be nicely relaxed by now, so once again your suggestions are building on a physical reality. Add to the relaxation suggestion the further suggestion that he feels incapable of activity, a state which tends to follow relaxation naturally, thus guaranteeing the acceptance of yet another suggestion.

At this stage, you might like to introduce a minor test into the proceedings by suggesting a number of times that he will find it impossible to raise his arm, then inviting him to try. If everything is going according to schedule, the arm should remain firmly where it was. (If, however, your subject *does* manage to raise his arm, do *not* conclude the experiment has failed. Keep talking calmly and quietly, reinforce the suggestions of deeper and deeper relaxation, inability to move and specific inability to move the arm, then try the test again a little later. Unless you have been singularly unlucky in your choice of subject, perseverance will bring you the results you want.)

Once you have carried out the test successfully, move on to the suggestion that your subject is drifting and feels miles away. Add to this the suggestion that he also feels a pleasant, relaxing warmth thoughout his body. You have now reached the realm of pure suggestion and any results you achieve will be unaided by the sort of physical tricks which reinforced the earlier suggestions. They rate a high 54 and 53 respectively on the Eysenck-Furneaux scale and you have, in any case, prepared the groundwork very thoroughly.

Have patience. The time taken for hypnotic induction varies from subject to subject and some go under remarkably quickly, but it is best to assume you will have to invest a considerable amount of effort. Repeat suggestions over and over, reinforcing their effect. Pay close attention to your subject, who will often give clear indications of how comfortable, or otherwise, he is with the induction process. If you are happy with progress so far, you can now introduce a second test.

In this test, suggest one of the subject's arms is becoming stiff and rigid. If reaction is positive, you may wish to test for glove anaesthesia, although you should recognize this as being more for your own reassurance than anything else.

Two important points arise here, both concerned with your responsibilities as a hypnotist: The first is that having given a test suggestion such as muscular rigidity, you must *always* be sure to counteract it afterwards, whether or not the test proved successful.

It is easy enough to remember the counter-suggestion if your subject has reacted positively — you can see the discomfort something like a rigid arm produces — but the situation changes when your initial suggestion does not seem to have been accepted. In such circumstances, you are far more likely to forget the counter-suggestion . . . and may even fail to see the need for it in the first place.

In fact the need is there because of a curious phenomenon which sometimes arises within the hypnotic process: delayed action response. This is exactly what it sounds like. Suggestions given during trance sometimes do not take effect immediately, but will be accepted by the subject later. Sometimes the timelag between suggestion and acceptance is quite considerable. I know personally of one case where a suggestion took ten days to bite; and another where the timelag was nearly eight weeks. Against this background counteracting a suggestion becomes very important if you are to guard against the possibility of a reaction at a later date.

The second point relates to the whole question of testing for anaesthesia. A hypnotized subject's inability to feel pain is sometimes very dramatic indeed. But this very fact brings its own problems. Without the warning signals given by a pain reaction, it is perfectly possible to cause tissue damage in the course of a test. Obviously this is something to be avoided; and it is also something which is *your* total responsibility . . . as is the proper sterilization of pins, needles or any other instruments you decide to use for a test.

Once you have successfully placed a subject in trance, your next problem is what to do with him. At this stage, I would recommend that you do very little, and certainly that you do *not* attempt any form of regression. As a first step, you are simply gaining experience as a hypnotist, learning the induction process and familiarizing yourself with the indications of the trance state. You might benefit your subject with a few simple suggestions — that he will henceforth be more relaxed, more positive in his outlook, happier, more fulfilled, etc. — but that is as far as it should go.

Bringing your subject out of trance is quite straightforward. Tell him that you are going to count to three. Suggest that on the final count he will open his eyes and that as he does so, he will instantly become alert and fully aware of everything that is going on around him. Tell him that he will feel relaxed, happy and invigorated, as if he had just emerged from a deep, refreshing sleep. (Avoid negative suggestions, such as 'you will have no headache'. The mind has an unhappy knack of missing that little word 'no' and obediently providing just the condition you wish to deny.) Having given these suggestions a few times, count firmly to three and encourage the subject to waken. Almost every subject will come out of trance on cue. For the few who are tardy, simply repeat the process. Very rarely indeed will you be required to repeat it more than once.

The practical task associated with this lesson is to find yourself a suitable subject and place him, or her, in trance using the method outlined above. This may seem a daunting prospect, but do please give it a try. Hypnosis is such an important tool of reincarnation research that the more personal experience you have of it the better. And this holds good, even if you plan only to have someone else hypnotize *you* for past life investigation.

I have to come out in the open here and admit that of the dozens — indeed hundreds — of people who have requested training from me, a handful failed utterly to become hypnotists. I have no real idea why this was so, although I suspect lack of confidence may have been a factor. Certainly the induction process is easy enough to learn and the safety guidelines both simple and understandable.

Perhaps the single most important factor in successful trance induction is not the hypnotist at all, but the subject. The time and effort you spend in searching out a suitable subject will be a worthwhile investment. Certainly there is no excuse at all for deciding you are not a hypnotist on the basis of a single experiment with a single subject. Keep trying with the same subject and keep trying with new subjects. Sooner or later (and probably sooner) you will find someone you can work with successfully.

There is, incidentally, no easy way of determining a good hypnotic subject in advance. The rule of thumb is that psychotics, alcoholics and the mentally defective all tend to be difficult to hypnotize, as are very young children. After that, you determine a good subject through trial and error. There *are* some preliminary tests you can carry out — stage hypnotists often use them to preselect good subjects — but none are infallible and you will be better served simply by attempting a full induction and seeing what happens.

Please do not go on to your next lesson until you have at least *tried* to hypnotize a minimum of three different subjects . . . or succeeded in hypnotizing one.

7.

Regression Research

*'I'm at the theatre . . . but I'm not watching, am I? I'm talking to you . . .
you know, I think I'm fuddled with gin.'*
— Edna Greenan regressed to a life as Nell Gwynn

Several years ago, an Air Force sergeant asked me to hypnotize him as an aid
to stopping smoking. In the circumstances of the request, I had no facilities for
treatment, but since his military training had inured him to extremes of hardship,
he readily agreed to stretch out on a carpeted floor.

He achieved a satisfactory trance level and was given the relevant suggestions.
As the session finished, a mutual friend walked into the room. 'Were you really
hypnotized?' she asked him. The Sergeant thought for a moment, then answered,
'I suppose I must have been, otherwise I wouldn't have been lying on the floor
like an idiot for the last half hour.'

That little incident embodies a telling description of the hypnotic state. For
most people, trance is thought to be similar to sleep, an assumption compounded
by the fact that many hypnotists (myself included) frequently use sleep suggestions
in the induction process.

But hypnosis is *not* sleep, and is not even *like* sleep. As you pass into trance,
you do not lose consciousness at all. You remain fully aware of everything that
is going on around you and the awareness remains, even in deep trance, unless
the hypnotist specifically directs your attention elsewhere, as in regression or
the sort of induced hallucination that persuaded the soldier to attack his superior
officer.

This is not to say hypnosis feels exactly like your waking state. It doesn't. You
find yourself very relaxed, very warm, very comfortable. Your mind drifts gently
and your body, after initial sensations of heaviness, can begin to feel quite light,
or cease to impinge on your consciousness at all. As the trance deepens, you begin

to think of yourself as a disembodied mind, floating and drifting through an inner darkness. But the most important change is that the voice of the hypnotist becomes the single most important thing in your life, and the urge to please the hypnotist becomes, in practical terms, irresistible.

The collective sensations are extremely pleasant; for some subjects almost addictive. When you experience them, you can understand at once that, contrary to popular opinion, trance induction does not involve a battle of wills. The trance state is so seductive that once it begins to manifest, it tends to draw a subject in. Sometimes its attractions are sufficient to overcome the most unsuitable circumstances.

Before she retired, Pan Collins was senior researcher on Ireland's most popular television programme, *The Late Late Show*. She was also, in her own words, God's gift to hypnotists. On one occasion when I worked to place her in trance, a heavily amplified rock group was practising in the next room.

'I kept thinking to myself, "This is really not going to work"', Pan wrote in her autobiography, *It Started on the Late Late Show*. But it did. Pan passed as easily into trance as she would have in a soundproof chamber. She also, since this was the reason for the experiment, regressed to what seemed to be a previous existence.

'Where are you?' I asked her.

'I am walking along a river bank.'

'Who are you?'

'My name is Cynthia Lambert.'

'What year is it?'

'It's the year 1797.'

This sort of opening is fairly typical of a regression experiment. Your subject is, so to speak, pushed back beyond the womb to 'land' at a random point in the course of a past life. On a first regression, there is no way you can select where the experience of this life begins. Pan Collins found herself walking along a river bank. Another of my subjects opened her eyes on a parade of elephants. Another emerged alone in the library of her Victorian home. The variety is endless. (You have more control during subsequent regressions. Once you have discovered some details about a subject's past life, you can then suggest directly where the next regressions should start.)

There is also some variation in the way regression is experienced. Regression of any sort is impossible until an acceptably deep trance level is achieved, but even so not everyone finds themselves reliving a past life in exactly the same way. For some, the experience is a little like a vivid daydream: pictures form in the mind unbidden, but without confusion with reality. For others, the distinction between inner and outer reality is less clear. The vision of a past life is much like a dream: real enough for much of the time, yet still sufficiently different for you to know it is not your everyday existence.

One of my own recall experiences (which actually did not involve hypnosis) was very much like watching a peculiar movie. It seemed as if a window opened in reality through which I could view a highly elaborate play. As with any interesting entertainment, I found myself identifying strongly with the action. But I never lost consciousness of the fact that I was not only an actor in that play, but also a viewer lying on a couch in another dimension.

A considerable number of subjects, however, do not experience regression in any of these ways. Their subjective perception is of movement through darkness, followed by a sudden plunge into a new, *wholly physical*, reality. It is, of course, an illusion, but the illusion is perfect. Following one regression session, I had enormous trouble persuading a subject he had not actually been where he clearly remembered being.

Running an efficient regression session is a matter of experience. We have already noted that where your subject emerges in the past life experience is entirely a matter of chance. Sometimes it is not particularly clear either. Joe Keeton's experience with Michael O'Mara bears this out.

'What is your name?' asked Mr Keeton. But the regressed O'Mara only muttered indistinctly, 'Thirsty . . .'

After the event, of course, we can see Michael O'Mara was reliving a portion of his life as Stephen Garrett when that character was in a drunken stupor. But at the time, the material coming through was confusing in the extreme.

As facilitator of a regression experiment, it is your job to direct the subject in such a way that a lucid picture of the lifetime emerges. You do this by asking questions; and on a first regression, the initial questions are:

Where are you?
Who are you?
What year is it?
How are you dressed?
What do you look like?
What is your occupation?

Simple as they sound, even these questions need some explanation.

Where are you? is meant to elicit the *immediate environment* in which your subject finds himself. This is the question Pan Collins answered with 'I'm walking along a river bank.' Later you will have to find out (if possible) the name of that river, the country through which it flows, the city, town or village in which your regressed subject lives and so on.

Who are you? hopefully gets you a name, although I have had experience of a few regressions which took subjects to cultures so remote (and usually so primitive) that names were not in use. In such instances, the question will sometimes elicit an occupation — soldier, fisherman or whatever — sometimes only blankness.

What year is it? can, surprisingly, be a minefield. Pan Collin's answer of 1797 was straightforward enough since, as Cynthia Lambert, she belonged to a familiar culture at a relatively recent time. Not all regression subjects do. Had her past life taken place in China, for example, Pan might have confused me by insisting it was the Year of the Rat. And had it taken place anywhere just a few thousand years earlier, the difficulties would have been seriously compounded. Over the sweep of its history, humanity has evolved a multitude of ways of subdividing time, not all of them comprehensible to us now. Worse still, some regressed subjects have no interest in dates at all; peasants and primitives will often fall into this category. They follow the seasons because of their importance to agriculture or the movement of game, but beyond that dates are as alien to them as the surface of Venus.

If you get a confusing answer to this question, you are going to have to use your ingenuity to establish a rough dating some other way. One possible approach is to try to solicit the name of a current ruler — King, Queen, Emperor or Empress. Another is to hunt for details of recent battles or other broad historical events. If all else fails, fashions in clothing or current technology levels can sometimes give sufficient clues to narrow down the possibilites. (Although you need to be careful to match technology with culture. Reference to a mains gas supply would strike most of us as modern — Victorian at very earliest. But piped gas was, in fact, available in parts of China as long ago as the fourth century BC) Like much reincarnation research, establishing even a rough date can be a question of patient detective work.

How are you dressed? is the sort of question that can sometimes produce important information, but may equally serve only to confuse the picture. Certain styles can appear in many cultures at many different times — the Greek tunic is a good example. And what do you do with the information that your regressed subject is not dressed at all? This happened during one of my own experiments and only careful questioning elicited the fact that I was dealing with a very primitive Egyptian, *sans* apron.

What do you look like? can frequently result in a very vague answer, something by no means confined to reincarnation research, since an individual's self-image is often very much at variance with reality. A good hint is to direct subjects' attention to their hands. Be sure to ask about skin colour (a white subject regressed to, for example, a negro existence will not feel any differently and may forget to mention colour) which is often a reasonably good indication of broad geographical location.

What is your occupation? In some instances, a great deal can be deduced from a subject's occupation. An armourer, for example, fits into a clearly defined time stratum irrespective of culture or geography. Go too far back and no one wore armour. Come too far forward and its usage has been abandoned.

Once you have formed a broad picture from the initial contact, you can then experiment by bringing your subject backwards and forwards along that specific lifeline. I often add another question to my original list, *What is your age*?, since this gives me an indication of which direction to travel. At the risk of sounding obvious, if your subject has regressed to that portion of a past life in which he is an ailing centenarian, you are unlikely to find out much more about his life by bringing him forward in time. Once you have an age — even an approximate one — you can fairly quickly decide in which direction the key aspects of the life will be found. Then it is only a matter of careful questioning before an overall picture of the life emerges.

Sooner or later, you will find you are dealing with a subject who has reached a *between-lives* state. The hypothetical centenarian of our previous example might be purposely directed that way, as indeed might any other subject. Or you might land in such a state with a first regression. I have had experience of several subjects where it happened. One of them described the state as a pleasant pink fog. Another gave a classical description of leaving her body at the moment of death. There is obviously a vast field of research in this aspect of the experience alone and you are welcome to engage in it. I have tended to avoid the subject in this course since my direct experience of the state is limited.

As in many other areas, there is no substitute for experience. It is safe to say that the style of regression experiments you conduct will be very much your own and the areas you explore will depend largely on the motivation behind the regression itself. My own interest is in establishing historical validity for the technique, so that my questions tend to concentrate on those aspects of a past life which might be subject to verification. But this is by no means the only possible way to go. You might, for example, be interested in regression as a therapy, in which case your questions would be directed more towards the subject's most personal experiences.

Whatever route you take, the first steps on the road are identical. You must persuade a hypnotized subject to regress. Which is exactly what you will be required to do in the practical section of this lesson.

Lesson Seven

You have now reached perhaps the most exciting stage of your course: your first direct experience of a past life. For the practical work of this lesson, I want you to set up a full-scale regression experiment. You can do this one of two ways: as a facilitator or as a subject. If you go the former route, you will need to find a willing colleague capable of achieving deep hypnotic trance. If you go the latter, you will have to find a hypnotist to put *you* under, and one who already knows, or is willing to learn, regression technique. Either way, familiarize yourself thoroughly with the material presented in the theoretical part of this lesson, and with what follows.

Set aside at least two hours for your experiment, and more if possible. Use a warm room with a comfortable couch or bed and try to make sure you will not be disturbed. Arrange to have a record kept of any material that might emerge from the experiment. This can be done by having the facilitator or a third party take notes, but an easier and more satisfactory method is to use a tape recorder. There is no need to record the hypnotic induction: the machine can be switched on when the past life regression begins. Follow the hypnotic procedure exactly as you have learned in the last lesson. Test for trance level and continue until you are satisfied that the trance has deepened as much as possible.

Once a subject has achieved a satisfactory level of hypnotic trance, the technique of regression is very simple. While there are several workable variations on the basic theme, my own approach involves first asking subjects their age, then suggesting they are moving backwards in time to their last birthday. You then ask for a few details about what they were doing on the day. This is something that hardly requires hypnosis. Most people can remember perfectly well what they were doing on their last birthday. But this part of the regression does little more than lay foundations and allow the subject to become accustomed to the process as a whole.

When they have described what they were doing, you should then suggest they are travelling back to an earlier birthday, this time five years before. Once again ask them to describe briefly what they are doing. Follow this with a series of jumps, birthday by birthday, at ten-year intervals until your subject reaches childhood. By this time, of course, conscious memory is unlikely to play much, if any, part in the recall. Often a subject will begin to show clear signs of living the regression. As mentioned in the last lesson, vocabulary, tone and even behaviour can become increasingly childlike.

Continue with this deliberate, step by step process until the subject has regressed to his fifth birthday, then I begin to speed things up, suggesting that he is moving further and further back in time, faster and faster now, five years old . . . four years old . . . three years old . . . two years old . . . one year . . . six months . . . three months . . . and still back, back beyond the moment of birth, back beyond the womb and still further back in time . . .

This part of the regression differs from what has gone before in that it *hurries* the subject. This is quite deliberate. There are two great traumas in life — birth and death. Past-life regression, by its very nature, takes a subject through both of them . . . and does so very close together. While conscious adult experience of birth is interesting and experience of death even more so, both can be extremely disturbing to an unprepared subject. By using the technique outlined above, you blur birth/death impressions and reduce trauma to a minimum. (In my own work using this technique, few subjects are even *aware* of passing through the birth/death experiences. They feel only a sort of pseudo movement before their past life opens up.)

The more often you repeat the suggestion that they are moving further back in time, the earlier the past life your subject is likely to experience. This can actually be very early indeed: there are several recorded instances of regression to a prehistoric existence. Here again, only practive brings any measure of control to the situation, although it is as well to remember that once your subject has successfully recalled a past life you can direct him back to it simply by suggesting that he goes there.

With the technical part of the regression process completed, start the ball rolling by asking '*Where are you now?*' When your subject replies, follow through with the standard questions:

Who are you?
What year is it?
How are you dressed?
What do you look like?
What is your occupation?

But do bear in mind these are guideline questions only, set out to help you through your first experiment. Feel free to diverge from them at any time to follow up such lines of inquiry as the experiment itself suggests. Once you have established some basic information, you can then move the subject along his lifeline simply by suggestions like, 'You are now moving two years backwards (or forwards) in time. Where are you now?

Pan Collins recalled her experience as Cynthia Lambert when this technique was applied to her:

> 'Then he brought me forward a little bit in time and I was a little older. This time I was standing in the embrasure of a window in a large room where people were dancing and I could hear laughter and music. I was wearing a long white gown cut on Empire lines with a sash under the bust . . .'

The investigation of a past life, particularly the first time it emerges, is very much a hit-and-miss process. You may find yourself with a subject who is reliving an unpleasant or destructive experience. There are times, particularly in therapeutic regressions, when it is important to allow this to run its course, but for your initial experiment — indeed until you are fully experienced and comfortable with the whole regression process — I would strongly suggest you avoid such troubled areas.

Should you hit on one by accident your subject's discomfort will be immediately apparent. Simply suggest that he or she is moving backwards or forwards in time a sufficient distance to leave the trauma behind. Reinforce this with suggestions of calm, relaxation and freedom from pain, then continue with your investigations.

Occasionally you may stumble on a trauma so unpleasant that it resists all calming suggestions. In such (fortunately rare) instances, your only option is to terminate the session, bring your subject out of trance and reassure him that what upset him was only a memory.

If all goes well, you and your subject (or you and your facilitator) will have a truly fascinating session; and one that may well prove important. Do not prolong past life recall beyond an hour for the initial experiments, although you can lengthen this period, with your subject's permission, as the two of you gain in experience.

Terminate the session by suggesting that the subject is coming forward in time to the present, back to his/her current life, back to the room in which the experiment is taking place. Intersperse these with suggestions of calm and relaxation and, most important, with clear, repeated suggestions that your subject *will* remember everything experienced during the regression. Post hypnotic amnesia, which you learned about in the last lesson, is just as automatic in regression as in any other form of hypnotic experiment. Unless specifically instructed to remember, your subject will, in a majority of cases, fail to recall all or part of the experience.

Finally, keep the record of the experiment carefully. This may be your first regression, but hopefully it will not be your last.

8.

The Christos Method

'It is certainly a fascinating experience.'
— Gerald M. Glaskin, referring to the Christos technique

Two Case Studies

Frank M. was, before his retirement, one of the top professional business executives in the United Kingdom. His career, which included managing directorships in a number of Britain's largest manufacturing companies, was marked in its early days, by a rapid rise from the shop floor. Frank had the dynamism, drive and, at times, the raw aggression required to get to the top and stay there. Even compulsory retirement and the obligatory golden handshake did little to dampen his restless energies: he has now established his own management consultancy and is heading for a Doctorate with the Open University.

On a summer's afternoon several years ago, Frank M. lay on a couch in my study, eyes closed, describing a disturbingly vivid experience. He had found himself lightly dressed in a loincloth and carrying a spear, trotting along a narrow jungle path. He was younger, slimly built and brown skinned, but these differences were minor in comparison to one change which was so dramatic it compelled his attention. His sense of smell had become so acute he could track game by the scent traces they left as they brushed against the undergrowth.

He was, it seemed, engaged in tracking then. He had been travelling for days, maintaining a pace that would have been punishing for a modern man but which, for Frank's brown-skinned alter ego, was nothing unusual. He was extremely hungry, but thought little of that: he had been extremely hungry for much of his life.

I enquired what he was tracking, but failed to get a satisfactory answer. Frank

85

knew all right and was willing enough to tell, but he did not have the words. From his description, the animal sounded a little like a deer, except that it was not part of a herd. I did discover, however, that Frank and his tribe were not averse to a diet of shoots, beetles and grubs when they could not find anything more substantial. His favourite food, however, seemed to be goat. When he could catch a goat.

It was obvious Frank was recalling a life that was primitive in the extreme. If his people had discovered a way to make fire, they certainly did not use it for cooking. Meat was hunted, killed and eaten raw. Frank was a hunter and a good one, perhaps the best of his tribe at least in his own evaluation.

There was no way to determine where he lived. Again Frank did not have the words. One guessed from the way he dressed and from the flora he described that the climate was tropical, which narrowed the possibilities, but not much. It was quite impossible to place even a tentative dating. Frank had not the least interest in the year and there were no clues in his description. His brown-skinned hunter might have lived at any time from prehistory to the present day.

Frank was worried. Despite his dogged persistence, he thought he might have lost his prey. This was a serious development. Listening to him talk, you formed the impression that the margin between a full belly and death from starvation tended, in that life, to be narrow. You hunted successfully or you died, and nobody awarded 'Brownie Points' for the great job you did yesterday.

He was a highly concentrated individual, impatient with the distractions represented by my questions. He volunteered nothing. The businessman on the couch looked as civilized and urbane as ever, but subjectively he was something else now.

Frank came to a rise overlooking a water-hole. Tracks in the churned-up earth around it clearly indicated this was a popular drinking place for game. Although he was thirsty, Frank did not go down. Instead he concealed himself downwind and squatted, spear poised. He was waiting for his prey. How long would he wait? As long as necessary, he told me. It might be minutes, it might be hours, it might be days. His prey might never come, in which case he would die. The thought did not disturb him. He had settled to his task with a patience so all-embracing, it was difficult to comprehend.

Something slid out of the jungle to drink at the water-hole: a wild dog, thin and wary. We waited with baited breath for Frank's reaction. His wife Karen, who had listened to his talk of a beetle and grub diet with increasing nausea, allowed her eyes to roll upwards and murmured, 'If he eats the dog, I'm suing for divorce'. Despite the threat, Karen could empathize with the totality of Frank's experience. She had undergone something similar herself, and had been frightened by it.

Karen's career background was also in business. She was Frank's personal secretary before they married and was, by all accounts, fearsomely efficient. After marriage, she quickly discovered there was not nearly enough fulfilment for her as a wife and mother and consequently went into politics, which she combined with substantial charitable work. Against this background, it should come as no surprise to learn she projected strength, competence and self-assurance. None the less, when Karen took her turn on the couch, she underwent an experience with which she could not easily cope.

She found herself on a high place, forced to cross on a narrow ledge. Some distance out she froze, unable to move forward, unable to come back. Waves of vertigo swept over her. She began to tremble violently, hyperventilate and sweat, reactions which all manifested physically in her body on the couch. Her heart rate rose dramatically. She knew, with absolute certainty, she was going to fall. And if she fell, she was convinced she would be killed.

As Karen's panic peaked, I suggested she open her eyes. She did so at once.

'You know where you are?'
She nodded. 'Yes.'
'So you remember there is no real danger?'
'Yes.'
'Can you cope with the experience now?'
'Yes.' she nodded again. She closed her eyes, returned to the nightmare and continued edging along the ledge.

The remarkable thing about both these experiences is not that they provided proof of past lives, for in neither instance was there any possibility of checking their validity. What sets them apart from so many other reincarnation research case studies is that, vivid as they were, they did *not* involve hypnosis or trance. Frank and Karen relived those moments of high drama with all the reality tone my description might suggest *while in their normal waking state of consciousness*. The technique which allowed them to do so was something called the *Christos Method*.

The Christos Method is an important discovery if for no other reason than that not every subject is suited to hypnotic regression. In my book, *Reincarnation: Five Keys to Past Lives*, I gave four alternative methods which used no hypnosis; and while all of them are useful to some degree, the Christos Method is well ahead of the rest. Its origins are, however, obscure.

In or around June of 1971, the Australian novelist Gerald Glaskin was visiting some friends in Perth when he noticed on their coffee table an offset typescript publication entitled *The Christos Experiment — Introductory Principles*. Closer examination showed it to be No. 5 of a series of booklets published out of a remote location called Mahogany Creek a few miles away from the small West Australian township of Mundaring.

It did not look like a promising read, even for somebody wth time to kill while waiting for friends. It seemed all too obviously a crank publication, possibly sponsored by some minority religious group or cult. As Mr Glaskin leafed through it, he was confronted by sub-headings like *The Seven Bodies of Man, Soul Contact*, and *Preparations for the New Age*. They did not reassure him.

The booklet was, however, better written than most of its genre and, having nothing else to do, Mr Glaskin kept reading. He absorbed information on chakras, places and something called 'Atmaic Consciousness' before deciding to set the book aside. Then he noticed a heading which read, *A Method to Remember Past Lives*. He could not, he reported later, have been more sceptical.

But just then his friends, a husband and wife couple, entered the room and the wife (in his book *Windows of the Mind* Mr Glaskin calls her 'Joy') noticed what he was reading. 'I'd like you to read that,' Joy remarked. 'It sounds absolutely fascinating. A friend of mine tried it and says that it not only works, it's incredible.'

When Mr Glaskin heard the name of the friend, he was impressed. So much so that he decided to try the method a few days later. The author of the booklet claimed it not only produced experiences which revealed past incarnations, but also indicated solutions to problems experienced in the present life.

Mr Glaskin described his initial reactions to the process in these words:

My head didn't actually buzz, but I did experience an agreeable and yet confused feeling . . . Within a few minutes — I think two or three — there was a distinct change: I was . . . succumbing to a new feeling of my mind being within and without (meaning outside) the confines of my skull; not only that, but it appeared to be both a conscious and subconscious feeling. And there was no doubt about it, I was indeed completely relaxed. I might have been not so much just lying on the floor as *floating* above it.

As the experiment proceeded, Gerald Glaskin experienced something extremely odd. He had begun dimly at first, but with increasing clarity, to visualize a cathedral. Now as the experiment progressed, he became aware of a sort of dual consciousness. He knew he was lying on the living-room floor in his friends' home, but at the same time he knew he was also floating upwards towards his cathedral ceiling. 'Both experiences were perfectly clear,' he wrote afterwards. 'I was two separate yet undeniably connected identities.'

Like Alice's adventures in Wonderland, Mr Glaskin's first Christos experiment was to get curiouser and curiouser. The dual consciousness opened up into a waking dream, the sort of visionary experience usually only found in the lives of mystics. He entered a dark mausoleum. The air was dank. Moisture dripped from the high ceiling onto the cold stone floor and was carried away by a shallow drain. There were plain stone sarcophagi around the walls containing the bodies of his predecessors . . . and his own sarcophagus waiting for him when he died.

Directed by Joy, Glaskin found himself to be a tall (nearly seven foot) coloured man dressed in a coarsely-woven lightweight hessian robe embroidered with brocade. He wore a brocade headband, a sapphire ring, ivory earrings and small carved ivory ornaments pushed through the septum of his nose. They were insignia of office: he knew himself to be the elected leader of a remote community.

The community itself was interesting, housed in a conglomeration of small, white, circular, dome-roofed stone and mud huts so closely clustered only pedestrian traffic could move between them. At the centre of the city was a building taller than the rest, the leader's palace.

Now thoroughly absorbed by his vision, Glaskin entered the palace entry-hall, a cool pale green chamber. He dismissed the dozen or so servants who came to greet him and went on to a smaller antechamber in which was a stone desk and backless chair. On the desk was a stone tablet into which was incised neat hieroglyphic writing.

Glaskin felt himself to be in his late twenties and somehow knew that in this distant life he would live to about 35 or so, a ripe old age at that time and place.

'But then a strange thing happened. Having had this revealed to me, my mind, my spirit, my other self, 'overself', call it what you will, suddenly seemed to emerge and float free from the body of my former self, withdrawing to stand in the archway and look back at my former body as it still sat there in the antechamber, head supported on clenched hand like Rodin's 'Thinker' and that body in turn still gazing at the hieroglyphic tablet. At the same time I again became aware of being, in actuality, supine on a twentieth century living-room floor.'

When he emerged from his experience, Glaskin found he was aware of a great many details about his alter ego which had not formed part of the actual experience. He knew, for example, that he was unmarried, that he had special monastic schooling, that the locality had been somewhere on the upper reaches of the Nile and that he had spoken an ululating language something like Tamil.

Whether or not it represented a past life, he was not prepared to say, but it did represent something quite extraordinary. It remained vivid in his mind with none of the disintegration of a dream. Nor did it have any of the familiar dream characteristics. It was, wrote Glaskin, a fascinating experience.

Having undergone several Christos experiments myself, I can only agree. I am not a particularly good hypnotic subject and, while an experienced hypnotist can usually coax me into a light or even medium level trance, this has never deepened sufficiently to allow me to undergo a full-scale regression. As a result, any far memory developed by hypnosis has, in my case, been fragmentary and unsatisfactory.

Against this background, I approached the Christos technique with considerable interest, but little expectation. In the event, it worked extremely well.

I experienced the same curious bilocation described by Mr Glaskin, as if I were simultaneously in two places at the same time. One of the places was the floor of my living room, surrounded by a group of sympathetic (if somewhat bemused) colleagues. The other was an island off the Greek coast a few hundred years prior to the birth of Christ. The body I occupied on the island was considerably older than the one I was using in the living room although many of its physical characteristics — general build, skin colouring, hair colouring, etc. — were markedly similar.

There was nothing dreamlike or unreal about my Greek vision, nor was it, in itself, particularly interesting. But I did share Mr Glaskin's ability to draw on the memories and insights of two distinct personalities simultaneously. While this seemed normal enough at the time, it is remarkably difficult to describe accurately. The most striking characteristic is breadth of knowledge. You can get a flavour of what this was like by imagining you have access to memories from two distinct lifetimes, so that your insights are based on a combination of them both.

The nature of the experience was surprisingly vivid: I noted, for example, that peculiar clarity of light so many travellers have mentioned in relation to Greece. It also involved something I had come across only once before; and that in relation to a trance experiment which had nothing to do with reincarnation. On that occasion, my subject spoke of turning in a *new direction* — that is to say, a direction which did not exist in the physical world. Under the influence of the Christos technique, I too turned in a new direction and there found my fragment of Ancient Greece.

The technique which produces these remarkable results is a little more complex than hypnosis, but involves neither trance nor suggestion and so might be thought of as less suspect. To put it into practice you need a minimum of three people, one of whom is the reincarnation subject. The full procedure (which assumes you will be the one who conducts the experiment rather than the subject of it) is as follows:

1. Begin by having your subject lie flat on his back on the floor. Put a small cushion or pillow under his head so his neck is straight and he can lie comfortably. Have him remove his shoes. Socks, stockings or tights may be left on. In this position, the subject closes his eyes.

2. Have your helper begin gently to massage the subject's ankles. A light, circular motion on the ankle bones is what is required here. Until you actually experience it, you will find it difficult to imagine how extraordinarily relaxing this is.

3. After about a minute and while the ankle massage is still going on, place the edge of your curved hand on the subject's forehead so that it rests between the eyes, fitting snugly into the hollow at the root of the nose. In this position, it covers the traditional site of the legendary Third Eye of Oriental Yoga, equated in the West with the pineal gland. This location is the spot highlighted by the Hindu caste mark.

Once your hand is in position and with the ankle massage continuing, begin a vigorous circular rubbing movement which should be continued until your subject reports that his head is buzzing. Make sure he remains fully relaxed. If tension has crept in, have him take several deep breaths and go limp.

This concludes the physical aspect of the method, although in several experiments I have let the ankle massage continue very gently throughout the remainder of the session since it helps the subject to stay relaxed. Should it prove distracting, you can always stop it at a later stage.

4. The mental aspect of the method now begins. Instruct your subject to keep his eyes shut and *visualize his feet*. He should try to make this (and all subsequent visualizations) as vivid as possible, so long as the effort to do so does not spoil his relaxation.

5. Remember that your subject is not now — and will not be at any time during the experiment — in trance. He can communicate with you quite freely without adversely influencing the procedure. Have him tell you when he had managed to visualize his feet successfully, then instruct him to imagine himself growing two inches (about five centimetres) longer through the soles of his feet. He should try to feel the sensation of growing and see the result in his mind's eye.

If this process is already beginning to sound bizarre, I may as well admit right here that it will get a good deal worse. But stay with it: results are what count and for a great many people, results are virtually guaranteed.

6. Wait until the subject tells you he has managed to achieve Stage 5, then instruct him to return to his usual length. He should try to imagine the sight and feel of his feet returning towards him to their normal position.

7. Repeat this process at least three times — more if necessary — until your subject is fully accustomed to it and can visualize the peculiar 'growth' with practised ease. Don't hurry this: it is a very important part of the overall process and one that lays the foundation of much that is to follow. Wait each time until your subject tells you he has been successful. Your patience at this point will be amply rewarded later.

8. Now repeat the whole process, but this time your subject is required to *grow through the top of his head* then return to his normal size. If you have taken the time to run him properly through the foot process, this should be fairly easy. Once again, repeat it at least three times.

9. Return your subject's attention to his feet and ask him to 'grow' out 12 inches (30 cm) this time and return to his normal length. Make certain he has done this successfully before moving on.

10. Repeat the 12 inch growth and shrinkage through the top of the head.

11. Return your attention to the feet and now ask your subject to grow out 24 inches (60 cm). Interestingly, the fact that someone can successfully make a mental two inch stretch does not automatically guarantee he will be able to go further. Have him keep trying until he manages the 24 inch stretch (which should be accomplished in under a minute) *but do not have him return to normal size.*

12. While your subject feels has has stretched 24 inches through the soles of his feet, have him *simultaneously* stretch 24 inches through the top of his head. Weird though it may sound, some subjects find that as they start to stretch through their heads at this point, their extended feet begin to withdraw. Persevere until the two-way stretch is achieved; here again, do *not* have your subject return to normal size.

13. While at full stretch through head and feet, ask your subject to expand all over, as if he was blowing up like a balloon. Keep trying until he can feel himself extended beyond the limits of his physical body. We tend to think of swelling as associated with malaise or discomfort, but in this instance the sensation is very pleasant once the extension has been achieved.

14. At this stage your subject is, so to speak, out of his body. Despite all the effort he has invested, he should still be reasonably relaxed. You should now move on to the next phase of the procedure by asking him to visualize and describe his own front door.

This is quite an important departure and it is worth spending time to get it right. Have him imagine he is standing just outside his front door and facing it. Ask him to describe the door in detail. Make sure he does so by asking questions. You will want to know the colour of the door, the grain of the wood, where the letterbox is situated, what the knocker looks like, whether or not there is a bell and so on. Have him describe the immediate surroundings. Is the door-frame set in brickwork? . . . in stonework? . . . in concrete? Is there a window to one side? If so, which side? Are there any ornamental plants or other decorations? Is there a boot-scraper set into the sill? Is there a mat? Use your own imagination to keep the questions coming. Be sure to ask what he is standing on as he faces the door (stone step? . . . paving stone? . . . gravel path?) and what he can see above him when he looks upwards.

In my own experience, this is probably the most crucial part of the entire process, so take as much time on it as you need. Your subject is working with something very familiar — the appearance of his home and door. He should be able to give you a minutely detailed description and you certainly should have the patience to persevere until he does. There is one very important clue to the success of this part of the process — how long it takes your subject to answer your questions. If he struggles trying to remember, he is not doing it right. Fast, easy answers show he is mentally standing outside that door and simply telling you what he 'sees'.

15. At this point, you should begin to work to extend your subject's capabilities. Have him imagine he is standing on top of the roof of his home and have him describe from that viewpoint what his garden and immediate surroundings look like. Here again, you should ask as many questions as necessary to satisfy yourself that he is mentally viewing the scene and not simply drawing his answers from memory.

16. Now comes a tricky bit. Have your subject imagine he is levitating straight up in the air until he is floating above his home at a height of 1500 feet. This sort of height is meaningless to a great many people (since few of us *really* have the ability to levitate) so try not to be too pedantic about it. What you are after is a viewpoint established a considerable height above the subject's home.

Some subjects, at this stage, will have taken to the technique so thoroughly that the great height actually makes them nervous. I had one experience in which the subject, who suffered from vertigo, broke out into a sweat. Should you find any of your subjects in trouble here, remember they are *not* in trance. All you need do is remind them they are engaged in visualization, not physically floating. Have them briefly open their eyes if necessary. A little reassurance will go a long way and you should be able to take them on to the next stage without too much difficulty.

17. Once your subject is on a holding pattern at 1500 feet, have him mentally turn around in a complete circle, describing what he can see as he does so. Encourage him to turn slowly and, as before, ask questions. You want to know what the landscape looks like from this height, what landmarks he can see, what activity, if any, is taking place on the ground.

18. Ask what time of day it is in your subject's vision.

Surprisingly, this question almost always gets a ready answer. Usually your subject will tell you it is daytime, although the actual hour may vary. Enquire about the weather. Here again you may get a variety of answers. Neither the weather nor the time of day need bear any relation to *actual* conditions. Indeed, if they differ from actuality, you may congratulate yourself on the fact that your subject's inner world is achieving greater reality tone.

19. If your subject has been describing a day scene, ask him to change it to night-time and tell you what he sees. (If the original scene was at night, ask him to change it to daytime).

When he has done so, ask him to change it back again and compare the two scenes. Generally, they will be day and night versions of the same scene, although it does not actually matter if they differ.

20. Ask *who* is changing the scene from day to night and back again. The purpose of the question is reassurance and for this reason it is extremely important. Your subject may be puzzled by the question at first (it sounds too simple to be true) but must eventually tell you that *he* is the one making the changes. Remind him that this shows he has total control over what he is experiencing and assure him he will remain in total control throughout.

This is a good point to remind him that he is not and never will be in trance during the experiment, so that he is free to open his eyes and terminate the experience at any time.

21. This is the really interesting part. Once you are certain your subject is entirely comfortable with this new imaginary viewpoint, have him shoot up still higher until he 'loses sight' of the ground below. Have him change the picture to bright sunshine (if that is not what he already sees) then have him come back down to earth and land feet first.

If all has gone well, he will land in the environment of a past life. This should not, however, be immediately apparent. A gentle transition is called for. Since he will presumably be looking downwards during his landing, ask him to describe his feet to you — what, if anything, he is wearing on them and so on. Then ask what kind of ground he is standing on and finally suggest he looks round a little.

From this point on, the procedure is almost identical to an hypnotic regression. Your questions should be directed to finding as much detailed information about the experience as possible, searching out dates, locations, names, occupations, fashions etc. which will be useful in validating the experience later. Make notes or tape record the session.

Since hypnosis is not involved, your subject can terminate the session at any time and should be allowed to do so without pressure. There is no special treatment for termination. The subject simply opens his eyes and calls it a day.

Lesson Eight

You have probably guessed the work for this lesson. Find a friend and a willing subject. Then, using the description fo the Christos Method as your guide, run the subject through a full session. Make a note of the results and, if you wish, repeat the experiment with the same or a different subject. (As with hypnotic regression, the same subject will not always find himself experiencing the same past life.)

When you are comfortable with the procedure, take a deep breath and instruct two trusted friends to conduct a session with *you* as the subject. Although there is no equivalent to post-hypnotic amnesia in the Christos experience, make certain that notes are kept or the sessions tape recorded for future reference. It is surprising how many small, but potentially important, details can be forgotten.

Conduct a minimum of two Christos sessions — one with yourself as the subject — before moving on to the next lesson.

9.

Alternative Approaches

'New interests are to be expected.'
         — Nerys Dee, interpreting the nine of diamonds

If you invert a tumbler on a polished surface, have four or five people lightly place a finger on it, then wait patiently, the glass will begin to move, apparently of its own accord. If you further place the letters of the alphabet, the numerals 0 to 9 and the words YES and NO around the table, the moving glass will enter into a dialogue with you, spelling out the answers to questions or originating messages of its own.

A variation of the moving glass is something called a *ouija board*, once almost impossible to find, but now readily available in many game shops. Typically, a ouija board is a heart-shaped piece of wooden board mounted on casters of ball-bearings so that it will move easily on any flat surface. You rest the fingers of one hand lightly on it and, if you are patient and have a certain, not uncommon, talent, it will begin to move without your conscious volition. Should you surround the board with letters of the alphabet, it will, like the glass, spell out messages. The name *ouija* is derived from the French *oui* and the German *ja*, both meaning 'yes'.

If you replace the ouija board's pointer with a pencil, it becomes a *planchette* and will actually *write out* messages without the necessity of alphabet cards. Both the ouija and the planchette have an advantage over the inverted tumbler in that they only need one person to get them going.

For centuries, a great many people have believed that the messages which come through devices like these originate in the spirit world. They may be right. Alternatively, the information produced may be derived from the minds of the people who use them.

Much of my youth was wasted on the investigation of the sort of mediumistic phenomena to which devices like ouija boards loosely belong. In the course of this investigation, two things became abundantly clear: some very odd things happen in this field of activity; neither traditional 'spirit' theories nor more recent 'scientific' scepticism really explain them.

This is not the place to enter into a full-blown theory of mediumistic phenomena, but it seems to me that in certain cases, material produced involves contact between the mind of the medium and the mind of the sitter. Yet this is *not* telepathy as that term is generally understood. A personal anecdote may illustrate the point.

A good many years ago, a friend of mine told me she had found a wonderful fortune-teller, a very old woman named Mrs Hamilton who specialized in reading cards. Mrs Hamilton, my friend assured me, had made a whole series of marvellous predictions all of which came true.

Naturally I could hardly wait to meet the wonder-worker. But there was a problem. Mrs Hamilton, who had once functioned as a semi-professional fortune-teller, was long since retired. (Mrs Hamilton is now dead. At the time she was in her late eighties.) She was prepared, occasionally, to read cards, but only for people she knew and liked. I asked my friend if she could set up an introduction and trusted to my native charm to do the rest. A week or two later, my friend phoned to tell me it was all arranged, although with no guarantees whatsoever that Mrs Hamilton would be persuaded to perform.

At the appointed time, Mrs Hamilton arrived at my friend's flat in the company of her daughter, a middle-aged woman of considerable reserve. Despite the fact she was forced by arthritis to walk with the aid of a stick, Mrs Hamilton herself was altogether more outgoing and lively. We hit it off from the start; so much so that she volunteered almost at once to read my cards, thus innocently sinking the elaborate plans my friend had drawn up to persuade her. She had me shuffle and spread the cards, but scarcely looked at them as she launched into my reading.

It was, as my friend had promised, an extremely impressive performance. She was able to tell me, for example, that I was married, that my wife was slimly built, tall and with short-cut blonde hair, that we had two children, both girls (the initials of each of whom she managed to give me on her first attempt), that our marriage was on the rocks and had led within the past two months to separation, that I was a writer by profession and had a considerable fondness for cats.

These samples are only a few random highlights from a torrent of information which poured from Mrs Hamilton. The reading lasted more than two hours and came to an end only because her daughter intervened, fearing her mother would over-tire herself. Afterwards I separated the data into two categories: material that referred to my current situation and predictions about my future. I was sufficiently intrigued to record the material and instigate an ongoing analysis over the next three years.

The picture that emerged from this analysis was clear. Where Mrs Hamilton spoke about my current situation, the overwhelming mass of information was absolutely accurate. Where she attempted to make predictions about my future, she proved without a single exception, to be wrong.

Although this experience can make no claims to scientific method or experimental validity, it continues to intrigue me. My friend assures me she told Mrs Hamilton nothing of my circumstances; and I accept this without reservation. It is, of course, possible that Mrs Hamilton investigated my circumstances through normal channels — by hiring a private detective for example — then fraudulently passed off the information as an example of psychism. But I find this impossible to believe. Mrs Hamilton was a very old woman who had obviously entered on that time of life when she felt the need to impress no one but herself. She read cards rarely and now that she had retired, flatly refused to accept a fee. In other words she had outgrown the motivation for such an elaborate fraud.

The fact that her predictions were so consistently wide of the mark shows she was no prophet. But if you allow me to dismiss the possibility of fraud, the remaining material certainly requires an explanation. The simplest one I can think of is that she somehow pulled it out of my head.

This, of course, immediately raises the question of telepathy. But experiments in telepathy have all involved *conscious effort*. You stare at a Zener card and try to 'send' its symbol to a distant receiver. You concentrate on a picture while your partner in the experiment tries to guess what is in your mind. Even the more bizarre experiments involve conscious effort as when experimenters work hard to influence the dreams of a sleeping subject.

The wealth of material picked up by Mrs Hamilton involved no conscious effort on my part whatsoever. I was not even thinking of the things she told me, let alone concentrating on them. But more interesting still, neither was Mrs Hamilton. She was a woman who knew absolutely nothing about telepathy or psychical research. As far as she was concerned, she just read playing cards.

On the face of it, fortune-telling by playing cards is a purely mechanical skill. Each card is assigned a meaning so that, for example, the appearance of the Nine of Hearts signifies an imminent meeting with a lover. This primary meaning is then influenced and modified by the context in which the card is read. To find the Ace of Clubs among several diamonds would signify wealth and an increase in social status. To find it among several spades denotes financial problems.

From this you can see that anyone with the patience to learn the meanings can read the cards. But this is not to say anyone can do what Mrs Hamilton did. She laid out the cards and promptly ignored them. Occasionally she might return to pick one from the spread, but as often as not this was only to assure me it did not have its traditional meaning in this particular instance.

It was very obvious that while Mrs Hamilton was aware of the set associations, what she told me had very little to do with them. She used the pack as a trigger for what was essentially a psychic consultation. It enabled her to reach into my mind and extract information about which I was not consciously thinking. In some instances she produced information I had once known, but subsequently forgotten and was forced to check out later. This information related to my early childhood and was subsequently confirmed by my mother.

Mrs Hamilton was the most skillful miner of the human mind I ever met, but she was certainly not the only one with the talent. Virtually every Spiritualist medium I know has the talent to some degree, as have quite a few people who do not consider themselves mediumistic or psychic in any way. Almost always, their ability is linked to some apparently disconnected device or technique, like

Mrs Hamilton's playing cards. Among these devices are numbered the ouija board, the planchette, the inverted tumbler, a technique called psychometry which involves picking up 'impressions' from physical objects, and even full-blown spirit communication in a seance setting.

All this has a lot more to do with reincarnation research than might be immediately apparent. To see why, we need to examine more closely what exactly is happening when you recall a past life.

One of the most telling objections to the evidence produced by regression research involves the problem of language. Simply stated, the problem is this: If you are regressed to a past life as the Emperor of China, how come you can't speak Mandarin? This is a perfectly valid objection and it is a poor response to suggest that certain regressed subjects *do* manage to speak languages with which they are not consciously familiar. For while this may be so, the number of such subjects is tiny. In the vast majority of regressions, subjects continue to speak in the language of their current life, whatever the language of the life they are recalling.

The real solution lies in the mechanics of regression itself. Techniques like hypnosis and the Christos Method produce such vividly dramatic experiences that it is easy to forget subjects have not actually *become* their former selves. This is easier to appreciate when you consider a regression that does not involve a past life. When regressed to early childhood, the middle-aged businessman on your couch may sound like a baby and behave like a baby, but it only takes a sidelong glance to convince you he is definitely *not* a baby. In exactly the same way, a subject regressed to a previous existence as the Emperor of China may sound like the Emperor of China, may act like the Emperor of China, but is, despite appearances, no more the Emperor of China than the businessman was a baby.

However bizarre the results, regression remains a function of *memory*. According to the new model of the soul we laid down in an earlier lesson, you consist of a pre-existent overself which creates a chain of personalities through a series of incarnations. The experiences of each life are absorbed into the overself, layer upon layer.

While it is natural — and sometimes even useful — to think of the overself as somehow being *out there*, it is really nowhere of the sort. The overself is actually *in here*, forming the bedrock substratum of your mind. It bears such a close resemblance to Jung's collective unconscious that I suspect the two may be one and the same thing, although Jung did not see the collective unconscious as a pre-existent entity in its own right.

Against this background, it is possible to suggest that you are equipped with two distinct types of memory. One is the databank associated with your present incarnation, which is gradually filled with the experiences of a lifetime from birth onwards. The other is the databank of the overself, which holds the collective experiences of your past lives.

Although separate, there is obviously a linkage between these two databanks. It may be the first actively transfers data to the second throughout your entire lifetime. Or it may be that the contents of the first databank are, so to speak, dumped into the second at the point of physical death. We simply do not know enough to do more than guess at the mechanics. Among other things, we do not know whether the information transfer between the first and second databanks is total or selective. If it is total, then the overself contains detailed information about the most trivial past life experiences. If it is selective, then only a précis is retained.

Should you feel it is stretching credibility to suggest you have sufficient storage capacity for a whole daisy chain of lifetimes within your skull, it is as well to remember that the adult human brain contains somewhere between 15 and 100 *billion* neurons. This gives it the capacity to store an absolute minimum of $2^{10,000,000,000}$ bits of information. Just to write out that number fully would require you to jot down one digit every second for the next 90 years. In more recognizable terms, you have the potential of filing away information equivalent to a maximum of 10 billion encyclopaedia pages. (Although it has nothing to do with our central thesis, I cannot resist pointing out that reincarnation theory provides an interesting solution to one of the great mysteries of evolution — why natural selection produced a brain with vastly greater capacity than, on the face of it, our species could ever need.)

Successful regressions do not send your consciousness travelling through time to sample the joys and sorrows of a past existence. What they actually do is provide you with temporary access to the databank of the overself. This databank contains a spectrum of experiences far more comprehensive and richer than anything stored in the personality databank you use in your day-to-day existence. But when you tap into memories of a past life, you are limited in what you can extract.

A computer analogy may make this clearer. You are in some respects like a personal computer connected to a mainframe, a large 'mother' computer. The mainframe, which represents the overself, has vast memory banks packed with data. The personal computer, representing your present-life personality, has far smaller storage capacity. Because of the link-up, the personal computer can extract data from the mainframe. But in so doing, it is limited by its own storage capacity. Thus the personal computer will always be selective in the data it extracts, seeking out only that which is useful to its immediate needs and ignoring the rest.

If I may carry the analogy a little further without, hopefully, becoming too technical, a further problem may arise due to the fact that the mainframe and the personal computer have different *operating systems*. Those familiar with computers will recognize this means that while data may be transferred between the two, the *structure* of the data has to be modified to suit the individual computer.

Language is, of course, an information structure. Consequently when you begin to extract data from the overself, it seems likely that it will have to be modified for use by your present personality. Thus, if you do not now speak Mandarin, past life information presented in Mandarin would be of no benefit to you whatsoever. In computer terms, it would be using an inappropriate operating system.

Using this model, we can see that the majority of regression experiences have been successful in translating past life data into a form usable by the present personality. Those few instances where the former language is recalled would actually represent a failure of the system, however much they might be welcomed by investigators.

Once you begin to think of regression as accessing the databanks of the overself, it is easy to understand that hypnosis and the Christos Method are not the only techniques likely to produce results. *Anything* that gives access to the deeper layers of the mind may, potentially, be of value . . . which brings us full circle to Mrs Hamilton's wicked pack of cards, ouija boards, inverted tumblers and the whole paraphanalia of mediumistic and psychical phenomena.

It is my experience that any or all of these things may provide you with valid information about a past life. They are far less reliable than hypnosis or Christos, but you may still wish to use them. If so, try to bear in mind that any validity they may have is directly related to the way they allow you, or someone else, to dig into the deeper layers of your mind. And, as in all reincarnation research, the data must be carefully checked.

Perhaps the simplest experiment of this type that you could try involves the moving glass. Any tumbler will do, so long as it does not have a stem, although you would be well advised to avoid using your best crystal since the movements can sometimes become sufficiently violent to throw the glass off the table.

Use a polished wooden table large enough to allow you to place the letters of the alphabet in a conveniently sized circle. A round table is slightly better for the job than one that is square or rectangular, since people are going to have to stand or sit around it. You can make your alphabet from squares of paper or card. Alternatively, a Lexicon pack does the job beautifully. Invert the glass in the centre of the circle of letters and you are almost ready to begin.

To get the glass moving you will need six people, including yourself. Six is an optimum number, based on my own experience. It *is* possible to start the glass up with fewer — as little as three will sometimes do the trick — but under six, results tend to be sluggish, unpredictable or both. With more than six people, the experiment becomes physically unwieldy: there are only so many fingers you can fit comfortably on the bottom of a glass. Have your six people stand or sit around the table. Ask each to place the tip of one finger *lightly* on the bottom of the glass near the edge. Then wait.

How long you will have to wait is somewhat unpredictable, but if nothing has happened after 20 minutes, you would be well advised to call off the experiment and try again another day, preferably with different people. If all goes well, however, the glass will eventually begin to move.

Initial movements will be no more than light tremours. Soon after these develop, however, the glass will move across the table-top, typically in short, darting movements. Finally it will begin to slide to and fro in broad sweeps before (usually) returning to the centre. At this point you can begin your past-life investigations.

Glass-moving has always been a bit of a parlour game and those of you who have already tried it will be well aware that the glass quickly develops a personality of its own in response to questions and that this personality usually claims to be a spirit of the dead.*

---

* Or worse. I had one moving glass which thought itself to be an alien from Saturn while another, with delusions of grandeur, claimed to be Satan!

You will naturally judge the validity of such claims for yourself. I can only assure you that the moving glass can often exhibit a curious talent for extracting information from the minds of those who operate it, hence it may be used with some justification for reincarnation research.

Using a ouija board or planchette is even simpler than using the glass; you need nobody there but yourself. (Which, incidentally, removes any nagging doubt that there may be a practical joker around.) In the case of the ouija, lay out your circle of letters exactly as you did with the glass, place the fingers of one hand lightly on the board, sit back, relax and wait.

You will be very lucky indeed if anything happens quickly, but if you have patience much the same pattern will emerge as in glass moving. the first indications of result will be small tremors in the board, then brief darting movements and finally strong swings across the surface of the table, with the letters used to spell out messages.

Both the glass and the ouija have a tendency to spell out garble when you first begin to use them. If this happens during your experiments, simply repeat the question and try again. If you stick at it, words, phrases and eventually whole sentences will finally emerge. During the garble phase, keep an eye out for fragments which are not garble at all, but mini-messages buried in a mess of random letters. Bear in mind that the devices you are using do not lend themselves to punctuation and unpunctuated messages are astonishingly difficult to read. howeasilywouldyoureadthissentenceforexampleifidecidednottobotherwith capitallettersspacescommasorfullstopsespeciallyiftherewereafewtypnigerrors threwnyin?

To use a planchette, you need no letters spread around, but you do need a sheet of paper for the device to write on, and experience will quickly confirm that the larger the sheet you use the better. Some of my best results have been obtained on one of those huge sheets of drawing paper artists use.

Technically, you start up the planchette in exactly the same way as the ouija board; rest your fingers lightly upon it, sit back, and relax. In practical terms, however, the planchette presents more difficulties than the ouija and only certain people can get it to work at all. Should you find your planchette stubbornly refuses to move, the best tip anyone can give you is to have patience. I know exponents of the device who are prepared literally to wait hours for results. Perhaps the most important part of the technique is *not* to concentrate. One medium I know achieves her best planchette results while reading *Gone With The Wind*. Select a book you find equally rivetting and see if the trick works for you.

The planchette produces what is known as *automatic writing*, a phenomenon which can be a fascinating study in itself. Just as the ouija and the glass often produce initial garble, so early examples of automatic writing can be something less than lucid. As the planchette settles down, however, the writing will usually become clearer and the messages more understandable. The handwriting need not — indeed *should* not — bear any resemblance to your own.

Some examples of automatic writing are freakish in the extreme. The planchette is perfectly capable of producing messages entirely written backwards, broken into lines, each of which must be read from right to left, or in mirror writing.

These things do not happen often, but you should be aware they happen sometimes.

Since this form of writing is *automatic* (i.e. produced without conscious volition) you will obviously not be able to ask the planchette questions in the same way that you can question the ouija board and glass. But you can *direct* the planchette towards a specific area of interest by clearly holding your *intent* in mind before the experiment begins. An even better method in my experience, is to *write down* your question ('What was I in my last incarnation?') before you begin. This is no guarantee you will receive an answer — planchette operations are very unpredictable — but it usually works.

Mechanical devices like ouija boards and planchettes are fascinating things to use, but when it comes to reincarnation research, you are, in each case, using them to reach into the deeper strate of your own mind. At this stage you may be wondering if a more direct route might be possible, one that employed no mechanical devices and avoided the complexities of Christos or hypnotic regression. We have already seen that all these methods do no more than awaken deeply buried memories. Is there no way of encouraging straightforward conscious recall? We can, after all, remember reasonably well what we did on holiday last year. Can we not learn to remember, in much the same way, what we did in our last life?

There are several published memory improvement systems, most based on visualization, association or both. Most will do exactly what they claim to do: help you remember just about anything you might want to remember. But as Harry Lorrayne, himself perhaps the most phenomenal memory exponent of the twentieth century, remarked: 'Most people forget things because they never make the effort to remember them in the first place.' Mr Lorrayne's system, along with all the others I have studied, is designed to teach you how to improve your memory *from now on*. In other words, they show you techniques by which you can make a highly successful effort to remember for the future. They do *not* show you how to improve recall of things you have *already* forgotten.

The picture is further complicated by the nature of memory itself. In her book *Total Recall* Dr Joan Minninger lists three distinct *types* of memory — verbal, visual and kinesthetic. And common observation indicates that elderly people often have vivid memories of their early lives while unable to remember what happened to them an hour ago.

Our commonplace exercise of memory and almost all the memory improvement systems are related to what I referred to a little earlier as the databanks of the present personality. Far memory, which brings us the details of our past lives, is related to the data banks of the overself. Because of this, even a photographic memory will not help you recall a single past life: it is simply associated with the wrong set of data banks.

If all this is beginning to sound like bad news, I should tell you that a method of far-memory training *does* exist, although it is difficult, time-consuming, and not at all certain to produce results. But if you are interested in trying it out, then you can certainly do so as an adjunct to your regular self-knowledge meditation.

Towards the end of your usual meditation period, try to imagine yourself *without your physical body*. Take, say, five minutes for this exercise. Continue, over a period of days or weeks, if necessary, to practise this act of imagination until it comes easily to you and you find no difficulty in entering into a state of being as a disembodied mind. Once you achieve this, move on to imagining yourself *without your imagination*, floating in a dark and silent realm of abstract thoughts. Again practise this over a series of meditation periods until you can do it successfully. Next and finally, imagine yourself without your thoughts. Nothing seemingly is left, yet *something* of you continues to exist.

This curious little exercise has the effect of bringing you closer to the overself, the essential *you*. If you persevere with it (although it is a lot more difficult to do than to describe) you will come to an identification with the overself which will allow you to tap into the databanks which hold the records of your past incarnations.

Having reached the state in which you are able to imagine yourself without body, thoughts or imagination, to activate those databanks you should then strive to sense the process by which you gain *experience*. Imagine yourself building up a personality and sending it forth into incarnation. As you do so, you will find certain images associated with the incarnation begin to arise. Note down the substance of these images when you finish you meditation period: they are pointers to far memories which are worth checking.

Lesson Nine

The various methods outlined in this lesson tend to be unreliable, difficult or both. Your practical work is simply to try out one or more of them and note down any results you obtain. But the lesson is optional. If you prefer to forget these methods altogether, please feel free to do so. But don't move directly to the next lesson just yet, because the time has now come for a little review work.

Go back to your earliest entries in your course notebook — the ones that related to your visit to any selected country in the world, your trip to some part of your own country and your selection of a costume from that imaginary store.

Read through the notes you made at the time, in association with the answers you gave to the questions in this Workbook. And as you read, look out for any pattern that may have emerged. You might, for example, note a tendency towards meeting the same sort of people. You might find the costume selection for you in the store was similar to the costumes of the people in the foreign country you elected to visit. And so on.

Although everything in those early lessons was fantasy, the fantasies were carefully structured to lead your attention in directions most likely to stimulate far memory. And any far memories that were stimulated would manifest in the fantasies themselves. This method of reincarnation research is far less dramatic than things like regression, but just as valid and, if analysed out properly and checked thoroughly, just as reliable.

Should you wish to pursue it further, you can introduce variations by noting your reactions to certain antiques, styles of architecture or even foods, then tracking down the time period and country to which they belong. All these approaches are actually no more than variations on a single theme — conscientious self-examination and analysis.

10.

Validating the Results

'Scientific proof of reincarnation, it is claimed, is no more than fifteen years away.'

— Joe Fisher

Perspective is a research newsletter published by America's Association for Research and Enlightment. The main headline in issue 4 of volume 9 reads:

PAST LIFE REGRESSION CAN BE ILLUSORY.

Since the Association for Research and Enlightment was founded primarily to study the teachings of Edgar Cayce, which very definitely include a strong case for reincarnation, the appearance of such a statement may have surprised some of the publication's more committed readers. But there was substantial justification for it. The article which appeared below the heading was based on *Hypnosis and the reincarnation hypothesis: a critical review and intensive case study* from volume 80 of the Journal of the American Society for Psychical Research.

The case study was carried out by the psychologist Robert Venn. It involved a 26-year-old subject who had been referred to Mr Venn for help with psychosomatic chest pains. The patient was to prove an excellent hypnotic subject and in the course of treatment a past life personality emerged. This purported to be Jacques Gionne Trecaultes, a French pilot machine-gunned (through the chest) during the First World War.

Over some 60 treatment sessions, the patient's chest pains gradually improved and he became totally convinced of the reality of his past life as a pilot. Mr Venn was far more sceptical. He analysed the wealth of detail provided by his patient and discovered much of it was accurate . . . but only where the information was available from local libraries. Anything that required to be checked from French sources proved untrue.

Mr Venn's patient had no memory of reading material about aviation during the First World War, but Mr Venn strongly suspected this was actually the source of his data. Essentially the same sort of objection was voiced against one of the most famous regression experiments of all time, Morey Bernstein's work in uncovering the past life personality of a Colorado housewife named Virginia Tighe. The story was told in Bernstein's book *The Search for Bridey Murphy* which became an international best-seller in the early 1950s.

Although the experiments were originally designed to test regression in the clinical sense (i.e. regression within the present lifetime) Mrs Tighe quickly recalled a past life as an Irish woman, Bridey Murphy, born in County Cork in 1798.

The regression sessions provided an enormous amount of detail about Victorian Ireland. Mrs Tighe talked about coinage, food, furniture, books, popular songs, farming methods and a good deal more. She was able to give the names of shops, Caden House, Farr's and John Carrigan's among them, and frequently used words like 'flats' (meaning platters) which, though current in the nineteenth century, were no longer part of modern usage.

Much of the information checked out. In one intriguing instance, she actually confounded experts convinced iron bedsteads were not in use in Ireland prior to 1850. Bridey claimed to have slept in one as a child and subsequent investigation showed that such bedsteads were advertised as early as 1802. Yet not everyone was satisfied that it originated in a past life. It was eventually discovered that Mrs Tighe had an Irish nurse in her own childhood and the assumption was made that much of the information had really been drawn from her.

Objections at this level are virtually impossible to meet head on. They politely avoid any accusation of fraud by suggesting that the information was absorbed *unconsciously* and regurgitated without the subject being aware of its source. This places the subject in an impossible position. We live in an information-rich society. Any one of us at any time may read a book or article the contents of which are subsequently forgotten.

But for all that, the sort of rigorous analysis applied by Robert Venn to his own study and by others to the case of Bridey Murphy is an absolute necessity. Hypnotic experiments having nothing to do with reincarnation research show the remarkable ability of the human mind to create detailed fantasies and role play within them.

During the three years I worked with a clinical psychologist, I witnessed this phenomenon many times. Subjects with no (apparent) acting ability produced stunningly realistic performances as sailors, farmers, musicians and, in one remarkable instance, a witch. In each case the fantasy was created spontaneously, at the explicit suggestion of the hypnotist.

It is also perfectly possible to inject into such fantasies information of which the subject is not consciously aware. I had a personal experience of this (in my normal waking state) while writing a novel a few years ago. The central character of the novel was an Egyptian Pharaoh whom I called Nectanebo. The character grew in my head for several months before I actually began to write, with the result that the creation was extremely detailed. I knew, for example, the era in which Nectanebo lived, the outline of his career, some details of his death and the fact that he had a fearsome reputation as a sorcerer.

With the fictional character firmly in mind, I began research into the history of Ancient Egypt in order to provide authentic background for the book. I was stunned to discover Nectanebo had actually lived and that his life had followed essentially the pattern I had created for him.

At the time, the discovery came as a shock. It was only later that I realized I had *already read* the same sourcebooks I was using to research Egyptian history. That had been some years previously and I had forgotten much of the content — certainly I had no conscious memory of Nectanebo whatsoever — but the relevant information had obviously been filed away in my unconscious.

If most of us are capable of role play and retaining information of which we are no longer conscious, then we are certainly capable of creating impressive, detailed, partly authentic but entirely fictional past lives.

The danger is particularly evident during an hypnosis session. It is characteristic of the hypnotic state that the subject will seek to please the hypnotist, often in very subtle ways. Most of those who experiment with regression techniques would be very pleased to obtain substantial evidence of reincarnation and subjects are only too well aware of that fact. The situation puts pressure on them to deliver the goods. If, for whatever reason, they are unable to find the genuine article, they are perfectly capable of creating an impressive counterfeit.

As you work to investigate past lives, it is your continuing responsibility to check out the material obtained. This is not always — indeed not often — easy to do: Pan Collins, whom we met in Chapter 7 walking along a river bank in the persona of Cynthia Lambert, quickly discovered this when she attempted to find hard evidence that her experience was based in historical reality.

Pan had many years' experience as a professional researcher and was perfectly familiar with the type of sources she should consult. In the records of Ireland's National Library, she found many references to Lambert families . . . but with very few exceptions the records referred only to the male line.

Male chauvinism is a fact of many historical records, effectively blocking detailed research into a female incarnation. In this and a subsequent regression which also produced a female persona, Pan was forced to fall back on circumstantial evidence — accurate description of period costume, the use of an archaic street name, the identification of a priest who performed her marriage ceremony and so on.

For a time this was enough to convince her the past life experiences had been genuine, but following a largely unsuccessful regression attempt with Joe Keeton in 1979, she changed her mind. Mr Keeton regressed her to early childhood, then terminated the experiment because he considered she was remembering the experience from her present adult viewpoint, rather than reliving it. 'So I think now that I . . . have never been brought back to a previous existence under hypnosis,' Pan wrote in her autobiography, 'because everything that I have said in any of these sessions could have come out of my own subconscious mind.'

It is probable that many of your own regressions will end in the type of frustration Pan Collins experienced. But there is a second, brighter, side to the research coin which can sometimes prove more intriguing and exciting even than the original past life experience. This, together with the fact that it pays to be thorough, is borne out in the fascinating case history of another subject we have already met, Pearl D., the woman with the recurring dream of the arena.

The first few hypnotic regressions undergone by Pearl D. produced past life personae which were unconnected with her arena dream. Then, without warning, one session produced something very different. 'Where are you now?' I asked her, having gone through the routine induction process. And where she was turned out to be very odd indeed. Pearl found herself in a Mediterranean setting, seated beside a blue mosaic tiled pool, wearing a short linen tunic and chatting to a few of the 40 or so friends who surrounded her. Her name, she knew, was Andreas and she was 20 years of age.

Identification with the Andreas personality was absolute, among the strongest I have ever witnessed in a regression session. Pearl lost all awareness of herself as Pearl. She no longer knew herself to be lying on a twentieth century couch. As Andreas, she even managed to integrate my questions into her poolside experience. When I spoke to her, it was as if she was suddenly enveloped in a transparent cocoon and had temporarily become, in some strange way, an observer of her own life. She heard my voice only in her mind and rationalized it within her cultural milieu as the voice of a forest spirit.

One of the early things I asked her was the name of her father. To her intense surprise (as Andreas) she could not remember. Lapses of this sort are not particularly unusual in regression experiments — access to the memory banks of the overself is seldom perfect — but can be disturbing to a subject who has, like Pearl, totally identified with a past life persona. Eventually, after a considerable struggle, she managed to recall she was the daughter of someone called Ado, but this was a family name (or possibly a nickname) and not the name by which he was generally known. She could not recall his public name at all. What she *could* recall was that he was the ruler of the country. She further remembered that her mother was Greek.

If Ado was king, did that make Andreas a princess, I wondered. Not exactly, Andreas told me. She would not become a princess until she was deemed fit. The rank was not entirely a matter of birthright: she had to prove her fitness. To do so, she worked with her father in the Law Courts. The rule of law was supreme in their culture.

I tried without much hope of success for a date and, predictably, failed to get one that made modern sense. But her description of the environment suggested an archaic era. I asked the nationality of her father and herself and after a prolonged pause was told they were Medes.

The waking Pearl D. was fascinated by Andreas whom she recognized at once as the woman in her arena dream. She readily agreed to further regression sessions, but suggested I direct her *specifically* back to the Andreas lifetime since this was the one she wished to explore.

Although initial regressions are random, once a past life has been established, it is very easy to return there if hypnosis is being used. The hypnotist runs the basic regression sequence, but finishes off by suggesting that the subject go directly to the past life in question. This Pearl did, time and time again. Over a series of experimental sessions, a very comprehensive picture of the Andreas life began to emerge.

Andreas could not at first recall the name of her country's capital city, although in a later session she identified it as Xanthus. But she was aware some sort of insurrection was afoot. From her poolside she expressed profound sorrow at the fact her father might be dead — a prediction made by spirits when she last visited the temple.

The mention of a temple visit prompted me to ask about her religion. What god did she worship? With some surprise, Andreas told me there were, of course, many gods. I pressed her to name one, suspecting an answer might give a clue to what period we were investigting. She recalled, with some difficulty, there was a statue of Mithras in the temple.

A description of the temple itself was far easier to elicit. It was small, dark and barely furnished, a building that would house a congregation of no more than 40. There was a fire on the altar and a well set slightly above floor level. When Andreas worshipped at the temple she would occasionally see pictures in the fire and believed on such occasions that the spirits spoke to her. It was in this way that she learned the death of her father, although the news could not immediately be confirmed. It appeared that Andreas' poolside villa was set on an island off the coast and the current disturbances made it difficult to obtain news from the mainland.

I was intrigued by the temple visits and wondered if Andreas was permitted entry because of her social status. Not so: men and women of any rank were permitted entry to the temple.

Further exploration of the Andreas lifeline produced material of high drama and tragedy. Shortly after the period by the pool, the death of her father was confirmed. He had been overthrown and murdered by his brother Pericles, a provincial governor who headed an open rebellion and installed himself on the throne.

Andreas herself was seized and imprisoned. For 18 months she lived in darkness. The cell was underground, cramped, wet, cold and smelling of filth. There was a hole in the door through which food was pushed once a day. It was not a healthy environment for anyone. For Andreas, who had been beaten before her imprisonment, it was to prove positively lethal. She had sustained internal injuries which had no opportunity to heal. A lung condition developed, with symptoms which sounded, to modern ears, suspiciously like tuberculosis. As the weeks dragged into months she weakened continually until she knew she was dying.

During the period she had only one contact with the outside world. A young guard captain, only a year or two older than herself, came at intervals to whisper news to her. He never came further than the doorway and seemed not to care whether she answered him or not, but his visits may have been instrumental in preserving her sanity.

Andreas did not, however, die in her cramped cell. One day, shortly after she was woken up, guards came for her. When they took her outside, she discovered it was already noon. She was blinded by the bright sunlight and unable to walk unaided. She was washed, her hair untangled and cleaned, then given a fresh tunic to wear. The guard captain who had brought news to her cell told her she was being taken to the arena. A military escort was provided, as much to help her walk as anything else.

From the captain she learned what was going on. Her uncle, Pericles, was finding difficulty in holding the reins of state. The coup he had led had never been entirely popular and now there was a ground-swell of public opinion running against him. Suspicion was growing that he had killed his brother, not simply replaced him. As frequently happens in such situations, the generalized discontent had gradually polarized around a single person. There were rumours abroad that Andreas had been assassinated like her father, not simply imprisoned as her uncle claimed.

As the rumours grew, the people had become increasingly uneasy and unmanageable. They wanted Andreas and it was obvious if they did not get her, further bloodshed might be inevitable. In a move to stop the unrest, Pericles had decided to exhibit Andreas at the theatre, thus proving she was still alive.

Pearl D. vividly recalled that Andreas, despite her weakness, immediately saw an opportunity in these developments. Her experience of the Courts had taught her that once a public accusation had been made, a full trial must follow. The rule of law was held in such high esteem that this would happen even if the accused was among the highest in the land. She determined at once to accuse her uncle of murder and treason.

It was for this reason that she had to cross the arena. Soldiers assisted her to the amphitheatre, but Pericles had ordered that she walk in alone, presumably to indicate that she was in good health and well treated. Thus, determined to accuse her uncle, Andreas forced herself step by painful step across the sand . . . And, as we know, failed. As Pearl D.'s recurring dream recounted time and time again, she managed only to reach the centre of the arena before her failing strength finally gave out and she sank down to die before the helpless, sympathetic crowd.

I have recounted the story of Pearl D.'s alter ego in detail not merely for its intrinsic interest but because it ably illustrates the pitfalls of validation research and clearly underlines the need for perseverance.

When I began the investigative process, I already knew that any evidence I might gather would almost certainly be circumstantial. Pearl D. had presented sufficient material at this stage to indicate that Andreas must have lived a long time ago in a distant land. I could not, like Pan Collins, slip down to the National Library or look up Parish Records under A. Since there was no clear indication of a date, we might well be as much involved with archaeology as history, a notoriously difficult area in which to find conclusive validation.

Worse still, Andreas claimed to have been a princess — or at least a princess in training. As a rule of thumb, you may assume that the more obscure the past life, the greater the force of truth should you manage to find historical reference to it. A birth certificate for the drunken Stephen Garrett would go a long way towards validating Michael O'Mara's far memory, precisely because Garrett was a total unknown. But anyone claiming to have lived as Louis XIV would have easy access to details of the Court at Versailles so that material produced would have to be of exceptional quality before we could take it seriously.

Against this background, I began my investigations from the most obvious starting point. When Andreas was speaking of her father, I asked their country of birth and received the one-word answer *Medes*. This is the name of a race, not a place. There is biblical reference to 'the laws of the Medes and Persians' which were considered in ancient times to be immutable.

This looked like a good start. Andreas had made much of the fact that to her people the rule of law was everything and not even a king was placed above it. What I had at first taken for a Greek or other Mediterranean setting might actually have been almost anywhere in the Middle East. I sought to find out more about Media, the country where Andreas claimed to have been born.

Media appears on no modern maps. The country lay in what is now northwestern Iran, roughly corresponding to Kurdistan, Azerbaijan and parts of Kermanshah. At the time I investigated, no written records from Media itself had ever been discovered and even Median artefacts were rare so that little enough was known of its political structures or religious beliefs. Its linkage with ancient Persia was well known, so there might be an inference of some cultural interchange.

This was actually borne out by another regression detail, Andreas' description of a perpetual flame on the altar of her temple. The earliest known religion of Persia involved a type of fire worship and it might be reasonable to suppose the faith had crossed the border. But promising though the line of investigation looked, this was where it petered out (or perhaps 'stopped abruptly' might be a better term).

One of the first problems to arise was geographical. The vast bulk of ancient Media lay inland. It had only a small stretch of coastline, fronting the Caspian Sea. But analysis of the Andreas material clearly showed she was describing a highly developed maritime culture with considerable emphasis on sea trade. However little we know of Media from written sources, that tiny coastline would certainly have precluded the sort of development Andreas described.

Despite an interesting 'hit' with her altar flame, I also felt there were serious problems with Andreas' description of her temple religion. I was aware of Mithras as a Roman god, associated with bull sacrifice rather than fire. The Mithraic Cult was military, hence predominantly (and possibly exclusively) masculine. There were almost no points of contact between what I knew of it and what Andreas described.

Then too there was the question of Xanthus which, as a captial city, should have been easy to track down. But no reference to Media mentioned it. Despite very thorough research, it was as if Xanthus had never existed. Furthermore, no capital city of Media occupied the sort of geographical location Andreas had described for Xanthus.

At this point, it is possible to see the sort of detail required for the investigation of regression material. It is also, I suspect, all too easy to conclude that however vivid Pearl D.'s 'Median' experience, it was not a genuine far memory. All the evidence so far unearthed pointed to a fictional construct, a fantasy put together using half remembered fragments of ancient history. And since Pearl D. had a scientific rather than classical education, the discrepancies become perfectly understandable.

But if this conclusion is reasonable, it also proved to be just plain wrong.

Lesson Ten

Although you do not, of course, have access to the full Andreas material which Pearl D. and I used as the basis for our research, enough information has already been given to allow you to engage in a little research of your own. And that research is your practical task for this lesson.

Read through the story of Andreas very carefully. Remember that my own initial efforts came to nothing and try to work out an alternative approach that might prove more fruitful. When you think you have found one, visit your local library and try to check it out. An encyclopaedia is a good place to start, but you may do even better by consulting historical or archaeological works on the ancient world.

If you draw a blank, don't worry; the mystery *has* a solution and that solution is given in your next lesson. But do try to dig it out for yourself. The work will make excellent practice in a situation where you already *know* there is something more to find.

11.

Establishing Your Proof

'Reincarnation is making a comeback.'

— from a lapel badge seen in the UK

Psychologists who used regression for investigations which had nothing to do with reincarnation were among the first to recognize how difficult it was to be certain that the material produced was valid. In the early days, patients were simply asked to remember certain events which had occurred at an early stage of their lives and relatives subsequently asked for confirmation.

But even where confirmation was forthcoming, it was all too obvious that the whole process was too uncontrolled, too open to falsification to be of much evidential value. Professor Eysenck put it clearly, 'The alleged events which the hypnotized person experiences under regression may have been discussed with him by other people long after they had in fact happened; the memories of the witnesses may themselves be affected by the story told by the subject who is being regressed; also, certain confirmative details may be elaborated by the experimenter to the exclusion of items that had not fitted in.'

What to do about this unsatisfactory state of affairs remained a puzzle for years, although the answer, in retrospect, proved obvious. It involved finding an objective fact well known to the subject at the age to which he had regressed, but which would certainly have been forgotten by him in the years that followed.

One fact that fits these criteria is the day of the week on which a childhood birthday fell. When you were six years old, your birthday was of even more importance to you than it is today. You knew then what day of the week the party would be held. But a year later, you would probably have forgotten and ten years later, you would certainly have forgotten. Thus, the validity of your initial regression technique can be checked by bringing your subject back to a particular birthday and simply asking him what day of the week it is. Interestingly, tests have shown correct answers from 93 per cent of subjects regressed to the age of 10, from 82 per cent regressed to the age of seven, and 69 per cent regressed to the age of four.

But it need not end there. The test can be applied to *past-life* regressions as well . . . but only sometimes. The problem is the one we noted in an earlier lesson when we discussed the question of finding an accurate date for a past life. Subjects can regress to any country in any era, thus making a huge difference to the way they measure time.

Many ancient peoples, notably the Babylonians, based their calendars on the cycles of the moon. Lunar measurement of the years has been preserved in Jewish, Moslem and Chinese calendars to this day. The Egyptians, by contrast, used a solar calendar, partly because of the importance of the sun in their religion and partly due to their agricultural dependence on the rising of the Nile, a seasonal phenomenon closely associated with the solar cycle.

Our own calendar derived from Rome, which itself had a chequered history of time measurement. Roman months were based on lunar cycles and the way each one was determined actually gave us the word *calendar*. Priests called *pontifices* watched the night skies for the first appearance of a lunar crescent so they could declare the beginning of a new month. When they saw it, the first day was shouted from the steps of the Capitol. In Latin, this calling is termed *kalendae* the epistemological root of our own word *calendar*.

The problem with lunar measurement, however, is that the lunar cycle is not a whole number of days. It is actually 29.53059 days long. An earth orbit around the sun is not a whole number of days either: the figure here is 365.242196 (repeating). You do not have to be much of a mathematician to work out that 12 (lunar) months are short a full year, while 13 months are too many.

To complicate things still further, our seven day week is not even vaguely based on astronomical constants, but has religious roots. It is derived from the Hebro-Christian tradition that God created the world in six days and rested on the seventh. While useful as a memorial for the devout, a seven-day week does not divide evenly into either the solar or lunar cycles.

The earliest Roman calendar, which was lunar/solar based began to show increasing discrepancies over the centuries. By the time of Julius Caesar it was wildly — and very noticeably — in error. The astronomer Sosigenes of Alexandria had introduced the more accurate Egyptian solar calendar to Rome and Caesar himself ordered its adoption for official Roman use in 45 BC.

This Julian calendar, as it is now called, was based on a calculation of the solar year at 365.25 days. This year was divided into 12 months which were decidedly *not* based on the lunar cycle. Like our present calendar, 11 of them boasted either 30 or 31 days, while the twelfth had only 28. But there the resemblance ended since the year began in March and ended in February. The Latin *septem, octo, novem,* and *decem* (seven, eight, nine and ten) were pressed into service as names for months (September, October, November, December) making a great deal more sense than they do today. Julius Caesar had a month (July) named after him as, later, did Augustus.

But while the new Julian calendar was a decided improvement on what had gone before, it was not perfect. The Romans were aware it would lose a quarter day each year and corrected it — as we still do — by adding an extra day to the twelfth month (February) every four years.

Unfortunately this correction was not enough. The Julian year was actually 11 minutes and four seconds longer than the solar year. Slowly, but with dreadful inevitability, the calendar moved out of step with the sun.

By the sixteenth century, the error amounted to approximately eleven days and became increasingly troublesome for a curious reason. The Christian religious calendar is based on the date of Easter, which assumes a fixed vernal equinox on March 21. Under the Julian calendar, this meant that the festivities were gradually shifting in relation to the seasons.

Eventually Pope Gregory XIII stepped in and instructed the German Jesuit Christopher Schlussel to undertake a full-scale reformation of the calendar. Schlussel adopted a scheme originally devised by the Neapolitan astronomer Aloysius Lilius in which the one in four leap year would be ignored unless the century year was evenly divisible by 400.

This sorted out the immediate problem, but did nothing about the backlog. To make the correction, Pope Gregory ordered that 15 October 1582 should directly follow 4 October, an edict which led to mob riots fuelled by people who considered they had lost 11 days from their lives. Gregory stolidly ignored them.

Since the new Gregorian calendar is important to reincarnation research, you should be aware that it was adopted by most Catholic countries, by Denmark and by the Netherlands in 1582. But the rest of the Western world was tardy in following suit. For nearly two centuries, you could actually leave England in, for example, 1679, only to discover it was already 1680 in some parts of Europe — and even Scotland!

Germany and Switzerland adopted the Gregorian calendar in 1700, Britain and America (then still a colony) in 1752, Prussia in 1782 and Russia, incredibly, not until 1902. France lived up to its individualistic reputation by first adopting the Gregorian calendar, then introducing a new one following the French Revolution, using this until 31 December 1805, then accepting the Gregorian calendar again.

If you find a subject who presents regression material from a country and a time in which the Gregorian calendar was in force, it becomes well worthwhile to apply what we might call the 'Birthday Test', although it obviously need not confine itself to birthdays. Take your subject to any important day in the lifeline — marriage, death of a relative, public event, etc, — for which a date may be elicited. Then ask the day.

Checking out this information involves some calculations which can be fairly daunting if you are not mathematically-minded, so to make it easy, I have created a home computer program which will do the job for you. The program is written in Applesoft BASIC and will run in its present form on any Apple II series computer. Changing the statement HOME to CLS throughout gives you a program that will run (although not prettily) on an Apple Macintosh under Microsoft BASIC, provided you use the CAPS LOCK key before making entries. If you use a different computer, other modifications may be needed, but the program is heavily annotated to make this easy. Either way, there is no need to type in any of the REM lines since these have been included purely for your information.

Screen displays assume a 40 col × 24 line screen with upper case (only) type, except for REM lines where upper and lower has been used for ease of reading.

The code is neither elegant nor particularly efficient. It has been written for clarity and ease of modification more than anything else. To make program logic easier to follow, each statement has been placed on a separate line. Since most versions of BASIC permit multiple statement lines separated by a colon (:), you may wish to group some of the lines together as a space saver. If you are an experienced computer programmer, you will certainly want to tidy the code and improve the screen displays which are more functional than artistic.

Reincarnation Day/Date Calculator Program

```
10   REM
11   REM Initialise program
variables
12   REM
20   BELL$ = CHR$(7)
21   REM [The statement PRINT
CHR$(7) will cause an Apple II
series computer to beep.]
30   DIM J$(7)
31   REM [Not really necessary in
Applesoft which permits
undimensioned arrays up to 10
elements, but may be required by
other BASICs.]
40   DIM C$(14)
50   J$ (1) = "SUNDAY"
60   J$ (2) = "MONDAY"
70   J$ (3) = "TUESDAY"
80   J$ (4) = "WEDNESDAY"
90   J$ (5) = "THURSDAY"
100  J$ (6) = "FRIDAY"
110  J$ (7) = "SATURDAY"
120  C$ (1) = "AMERICA"
130  C$ (2) = "BRITAIN"
140  C$ (3) = "DENMARK"
150  C$ (4) = "FRANCE"
160  C$ (5) = "GERMANY"
170  C$ (6) = "IRELAND"
180  C$ (7) = "ITALY"
190  C$ (8) = "NETHERLANDS"
200  C$ (9) = "PORTUGAL"
210  C$(10) = "PRUSSIA"
220  C$(11) = "RUSSIA"
230  C$(12) = "SPAIN"
240  C$(13) = "SWITZERLAND"
250  C$(14) = "OTHER"
260  REM
261  REM Opening screen display
262  REM
270  HOME
271  REM ↑ [Clears the Apple
screen and places cursor at top left
corner. Equivalent to CLS in many
BASICs.] ·
280  PRINT
290  PRINT
300  PRINT 'REINCARNATION
DAY/DATE CALCULATOR'
310  PRINT
320  PRINT
330  PRINT
340  PRINT "PLEASE ENTER
THE DATE YOU WISH TO
CHECK"
350  PRINT
360  REM
361  REM Get date↓
362  REM
370  INPUT "THE YEAR", Y$
380  Y = VAL(Y$)
390  IF Y < 1582 THEN GOTO
2000
400  REM ↑ [Don't accept any
year earlier than 1582.]
410  INPUT "THE MONTH (BY
NUMBER)"; M$
420  M = VAL(M$)
430  IF M > 12 or M < 1 THEN
PRINT BELL$: GOTO 410
```

```
431   ↑REM [Make sure a valid
number is entered.]
440   INPUT "THE DAY (BY
NUMBER)", D$
450   D = VAL(D$)
460   IF D > 31 OR D < 1 THEN
PRINT BELL$: GOTO 440
470   REM
480   REM Now check they've got
it right↓
490   REM
500   HOME
510   PRINT
520   PRINT
530   PRINT
540   PRINT "THE DATE YOU
WISH CHECKED IS:"
550   PRINT "DAY"; D
560   PRINT "MONTH"; M
570   PRINT "YEAR"; Y
580   PRINT
590   PRINT
600   INPUT "IS THIS CORRECT
(Y/N)?"; A$
610   IF A$ = "N" THEN 270
620   IF A$ <> "Y" THEN 600
621   REM
622   REM This routine has a loop
which prints out and numbers the
list of countries↓
630   HOME
640   FOR J = 1 to 14
650   PRINT J; " "; C$(J)
660   NEXT
670   PRINT
680   PRINT "PLEASE INDICATE
BY NUMBER WHICH
COUNTRY"
690   INPUT "THE PAST LIFE
WAS LIVED IN: " ;CN$
700   CN = VAL(CN$)
710   IF CN < 1 OR CN > 14
THEN 630
711   REM
712   REM Now check to make
sure the calendar was in force by
country↓

713   REM
720   IF CN = 1 OR CN = 2
THEN GOTO 3000
730   IF CN = 4 THEN GOTO
4000
740   IF CN = 5 OR CN = 13
THEN GOTO 5000
750   IF CN = 6 THEN GOTO
6000
760   IF CN = 10 THEN GOTO
7000
770   IF CN = 11 THEN GOTO
8000
780   HOME
790   PRINT "CALCULATING
. . . ."
791   REM This routine does the
actual calculation↓
793   REM
800   Q = M
810   E = D
820   K = INT(0.6 + (1/Q))
830   L = Y − K
840   O = Q + 12 * K
850   P = L/100
860   Z1 = INT(P/4)
870   Z2 = INT(P)
880   Z3 = INT ((5*L)/4)
890   Z4 = INT(13*(O + 1)/5)
900   Z = Z4 + Z3 − Z2 + Z1
+ E − 1
910   Z = Z − (7*INT (Z/7)) +
1
920   D = − (Z − 1)
921   REM
922   REM Display the answer↓
923   REM
930   HOME
940   PRINT
950   PRINT
960   PRINT
970   PRINT
980   PRINT "THE DATE
ENTERED WAS A"
990   PRINT J$(Z)
1000  PRINT
1010  PRINT
```

```
1020    PRINT
1030    INPUT "ANOTHER DATE
(Y/N)?"; A$
1040    IF A$ = "Y" THEN 110
1050    IF A$ <> "N" THEN 700
1060    HOME
1070    END
1997    REM
1998    REM This subroutine
handles date entry prior to
Gregorian calendar ↓
1999    REM
2000    PRINT BELL$
2010    HOME
2020    PRINT "CAN'T HANDLE
DATES EARLIER THAN 1582"
2030    PRINT
2040    GET A$
2050    GOTO 270
2997    REM
2998    REM Check America and
Britain
2999    REM
3000    IF Y < 1752 THEN GOTO
10000
3010    GOTO 780
3997    REM
3998    REM Check France
3999    REM
4000    IF Y → 1792 AND Y <
1806 THEN GOTO 9000
4010    GOTO 780
4997    REM
4998    REM Check Germany and
Switzerland
4999    REM
5000    IF Y < 1700 THEN GOTO
10000
5010    GOTO 780
5997    REM
5998    REM Check Ireland
5999    REM
6000    IF Y < 1782 THEN GOTO
10000
6010    GOTO 780
6997    REM
6998    REM Check Prussia
6999    REM
7000    IF Y < 1778 THEN GOTO
10000
7010    GOTO 780
7997    REM
7998    REM Check Russia
7999    REM
8000    IF Y < 1902 THEN GOTO
10000
8010    GOTO 780
8997    REM
8998    REM Start French checking ↓
8999    REM
9000    If Y > 1792 THEN GOTO
10000
9010    IF Y = 1792 AND M >
THEN GOTO 10000
9020    IF Y = 1792 AND D >
THEN GOTO 10000
9030    GOTO 780
9997    REM
9998    REM Error Handling
routine ↓
9999    REM
10000   HOME
10010   PRINT BELL$: PRINT
BELL$: PRINT BELL$
10020   PRINT:PRINT:PRINT:
PRINT
10030   PRINT "THE
GREGORIAN CALENDAR WAS
NOT"
10040   PRINT "IN OPERATION
IN . . ."
10050   PRINT C$(CN)
10060   PRINT "AT THIS TIME"
10070   PRINT
10080   INPUT "CHECK
ANOTHER DATE (Y/N)?" A$
10090   IF A$ = "Y" THEN RUN
10100   IF A$ = "N" THEN
HOME:END
10110   HOME: GOTO 10080
```

Before using this program, make certain the date you have been given really does relate to the Gregorian calendar. Anything else will obviously invalidate your results. The Jewish calendar is based on 12 lunar months which are 11 days short of a solar year, thus requiring a 13th month to be added periodically. The Moslem calendar ignores the solar year completely and works from alternating 30 and 29 day lunar months with the year beginning at different seasons over a 32.5 year cycle.

The following table shows when the Gregorian calendar was adopted in various countries throughout the Western world:

Country	Date
America	1752
Britain	1752
Denmark	1582
France	1582 (but abandoned 22 Sept. 1792–31 Dec. 1805)
Germany	1700
Ireland	1782
Italy	1582
Netherlands	1582
Portugal	1582
Prussia	1778
Russia	1902
Spain	1582
Switzerland	1700

Lesson Eleven

Your practical task for this lesson is to type the REINCARNATION DAY/DATE CALENDAR PROGRAM into your home computer. Or, if you don't run a home computer, to try to find a friend who does and who would be willing to give you a little computer time. (If he or she will enter the program for you, so much the better!)

Should access to a computer prove impossible, or should you find yourself working with subjects who provide data *outside* the scope of the Gregorian calendar, you are going to have to find more mundane ways of validating the material. In preparation for this, you might like to do a little advance work in getting yourself organized. List the various research sources in your district — libraries, universities, even friends with encyclopaedias or specialist books.

Meanwhile, you should by now have discovered there was more to Pearl D.'s Andreas material than seemed apparent to me when I first researched it. However your own researches went, you may be interested in comparing them with what happened following the original experiments.

I was not, of course, the only one carrying out research. Pearl D. was herself fascinated by the material and determined to discover how much, if any, of it was genuine. Interestingly, her research starting point was different from my own. She began not with the race of Medes, but with the city Xanthus.

She discovered at once, as I had done, that Xanthus had never been the capital of Media. Nor, so far as she could find, had there been any Median city of that name. At this point, however, she moved away in a totally different direction from my own research by attempting to discover if there had been a Xanthus city *anywhere*.

What emerged was fascinating. There was indeed an ancient Xanthus. Its modern name is Kinik, but it was formerly the principal city of a country called Lycia, situated above the mouth of the Xanthus River (now named the Koca) in what is today the Antalya province of Turkey. Although none of its Bronze Age remains had yet been found, Xanthus was mentioned in early Lycian inscriptions and reappeared in historical records of the sixth century BC.

What little is known of the city's history is dramatic. In 540 BC., General Harpagus laid siege to it on behalf of his Persian king Cyrus. The Lycian men promptly burned to death their wives, children and slaves, destroyed their treasure, then attacked the Persian army in a suicide mission which resulted in the death of every Xanthus male. But Xanthus itself was soon rebuilt and flourished until 42 BC when it was more or less obliterated by the Romans. The discovery of an historical Xanthus was more than enough to reopen our inquiries and point a whole new direction. It was to prove far more fruitful than my own initial inquiries.

Media was, as we had already discovered, part of the ancient Persian Empire and the Medes were, essentially, a Persian people. When Harpagus conquered the stubborn Xanthusians Lycia became a vassal state of Persia and Median colonists (among others) moved in. Later the country was again to become independent, although still nominally under Persian rule, and there was a growing Greek influence in its culture.

It seemed clear that while Andreas considered herself a Mede by nationality, the country she was describing was, in fact, Lycia. And if Media was largely landlocked, ancient Lycia had a substantial stretch of coastline, giving credence to the material which referred to its maritime economy.

In her account of her life, Andreas told of a rebellion against her father, the king who was murdered by his own brother. While nothing of this sort seems to have occurred in Media, historical accounts show that somewhere around 400 BC, there was, in fact, a satrap (provincial governor) rebellion in Lycia. This rebellion was led by someone named Pericles, the name Andreas gave to her uncle. He ascended the throne and ruled for about 18 years from the beginning of the third century BC.

My recollections of the Mithraic Cult proved only partially correct when checked against historical sources. Mithras was not an indigenous Roman god, but one of many absorbed into the Roman pantheon as the Empire expanded. This incorporation occurred at a later time than Andreas seemed to be describing. In Rome, the Cult of Mithras took on a martial air, but in its original form it was a Persian development involving fire worship and open to both men and women. Archaeological evidence has shown that Mithraic temples were invariably very small. According to our sources, none had ever been discovered that would have held a congregation of more than 100. The well mentioned by Andreas was also an invariable feature.

12.

Reincarnation and Evolution

'It is not enough to know about reincarnation; we must live it.'
— Guenther Wachsmuth

On 12 November 1966, readers of *Komsomolskaya Pravda* were treated to a story so bizarre it must have strained credulity to breaking point. The writer, Comrade A. Tsipko, told how he had visited the Moscow studio of Dr Vladimir L. Raikov and there met the great Renaissance painter Raphael of Urbino reincarnated in the body of a young female student.

'Can you tell me what year this is?' asked Comrade Tsipko.

'Why, 1505, of course.'

Comrade Tsipko began to take photographs. As he did so, Dr Raikov asked the student if she knew what her visitor was using. She did not, claiming the camera was an unfamiliar device to her. When Tsipko spoke to her about 'Sixties developments — the topic of sputniks was one thing that came to mind — she actually became angry and accused him of 'bothering her with nonsense'.

Ira, the student, was not the only reincarnation of Raphael in the studio. Three others all claimed to be inhabited by the same historical personality. None of the students involved had undergone regression. They were the subjects of a unique series of experiments in what became known as *artificial* reincarnation.

Artificial reincarnation involves a style of hypnosis somewhat different from the normal. Raikov calls it *active* or *dynamic trance*. EEG and other tests indicate that it is a state of super wakefulness which shows none of the alpha patterns usually associated with hypnosis.

The past life personalities were deliberately induced. That is to say Raikov *specifically instructed* his volunteers to become Raphael, or any one of several other personalities including the great Russian painter Ilya Repin and Queen Elizabeth I of England. No attempt was made to discover whether the reincarnated personalities were able to give accurate information about their historical period or, indeed, to determine whether the personalities themselves bore any real resemblance to their historical counterparts.

From this, it is fairly obvious that the phenomenon of artificial reincarnation has little in common with the process of reincarnation which has been the subject of this book. But for all that, Raikov's experiments are both interesting and relevant to our present study. Dr Raikov discovered that if he 'reincarnated' a great artist in his volunteers, it dramatically improved their drawing skills!

This is borne out by, among many others, the case of Alla, a physics student at Moscow University who was not, at first, particularly interested in art. Nor had she the least talent for drawing as early examples of her work clearly showed. She was, however, interested in Raikov's experiments and presented herself as a volunteer. She became one of those in whom Dr Raikov incarnated Repin. The induction process included the suggestion that Repin's talent was at Alla's command.

Typically, Dr Raikov permitted a reincarnation to last an entire afternoon. Soon after the sessions started, Alla began to draw noticeably better. After ten inductions she developed a desire to draw on her own time and took to carrying a sketch pad. By the time a 25 session course was finished, she had reached the standard of a competent professional illustrator and was seriously considering abandoning physics for a career in commercial art.

Dr Raikov did not confine himself to reincarnating masters of the graphic arts. One student was taken over by the great violinist Fritz Kreisler and true to pattern showed a marked increase in musical ability.

The most interesting aspect of the experiments was that the developed talent was *permanent*. It endured after the sessions finished and after the experimental series ended. Analysis of results suggested it took only about ten reincarnation sessions to stabilize a developed talent, which then lasted indefinitely. Students did not end up painting like Repin or playing as well as Kreisler, but their own individual talent was increased to a remarkable degree, far more and in far shorter a time than would have been possible by conventional methods.

Dr Raikov's experiments did not end with the development of artistic talents, spectacular though his successes in that field undoubtedly were. He explored the possibility of using artificial reincarnation as *therapy*. Several of his experiments in this field were even more bizarre than anything he attempted with his art students.

In one case he treated a middle-aged alcoholic by reincarnating in him the personalities of his own mother, his daughter, his wife and various other members of his family. The idea was to give the man a series of differing perspectives on his drinking habit.

This study underlines the dramatic differences between artifical reincarnation and the real thing. Many of the personalities manifesting in the body of Boris, the alcoholic, were those of people still very much alive. Yet the underlying *mechanics* of the two processes have much in common, notably that both appear to involve the temporary takeover of a body by a different personality. What Raikov discovered was that such a takeover can produce profound and far-reaching changes in the *current* personality.

Changes of this sort can be even more dramatic following a successful regression. The Canadian fashion model Bonnie Brown suffered from recurrent winter attacks of bronchitis from childhood until the age of 29 when she was cured by hypnotic suggestion following past-life recall.

The past life in question was that of a young East European sometime during the Second World War. The incident which started the trouble arose out of her transportation to a concentration camp in a freezing train without food or water. The journey lasted several days and ended with a vivid far memory of the girl standing by the barbed wire coughing blood.

'No one seemed to care. I was coughing and coughing until the end,' Ms Brown told her therapist Beverly Janus, who then suggested she would no longer be affected by the experiences of this distant past. The therapy worked. Since 1972, when the regression session took place, the bronchitis disappeared.

If this were an isolated instance, it might be dismissed. But it is nothing of the sort. We have already quoted Dr Guirdham's conviction that virtually every illness has a past life component and a growing industry in therapeutic regression has emerged in the United States. For some subjects, such regression has led to cures where more orthodox techniques have failed.

Shirley Kleppe-Moran, for example, was the victim of seizures which defied diagnosis or treatment. When they struck, they would last anywhere from 15 minutes to an hour. After suffering this condition for some 20 years, she presented herself to Dr Wambach, whom we met in an earlier lesson. Hypnotic regression produced memories of a life in sixteenth century Normandy where, suspected of witchcraft, she jumped to her death from a cliff in an attempt to escape pursuit. Reliving this unpleasant death brought an end to her present-life seizures.

It might be argued that both bronchitis and seizures could have a psychosomatic element. But not every case does. During the 1982 conference of the Association of Past Life Research and Therapy in Los Angeles, Dr Edith Fiore stated, 'There isn't a single physical problem that can't be resolved by good past-life treatment'. She should know, since her own past-life treatment was successful in resolving cancer.

The patient was a woman in her mid thirties who had undergone a dozen operations for bone cancer. In the regressed state, she recalled a life as priestess of an ancient cult which practised human sacrifice. Part of her role was to drink human blood. The recall of this repulsive lifetime acted as a catharsis. When blood tests were taken prior to her next scheduled operation, she was found to be clear of cancer, a remission which seems to have endured.

Two separate mechanisms appear to be at work here. Dr Raikov's experiments in artificial reincarnation suggest that when a personality 'takes over' a subject's body (as very often happens during a regression session) skills and talents associated with that personality overspill into the present lifetime. The experiences of past life therapists indicate far memory can function in a way similar to psychoanalysis and/or abreaction, but far more powerfully, so that physical as well as psychiatric ailments are often relieved.

My own experience in this field of work leads me to believe there is also a rather less specialized effect. Queen Elizabeth of Austria once remarked, "Whatever is of value in us, we bring from our previous lives that were spiritual." This I think is largely true, but to understand it we need to return to our fundamental model of the reincarnation process.

You will recall that this process begins with the overself, a pre-existent entity on a level of being other than the physical. This entity, the essential *you*, needs experience of the physical world in order to evolve and so sends an aspect of itself into incarnation. This aspect — essentially a dynamic personality seed — grows and changes in relation to its circumstances, taking on an imprint of the particular lifetime. At death, the personality is withdrawn and the related experiences absorbed into the overself, incorporated, so to speak, in the major memory-banks. The overself (presumably) ruminates a little on the experience, then sends out another personality seed and the process repeats.

This model is, of course, simplistic. The impression is given that the overself is somehow 'locked out' of physical experience until the body dies and the personality is reabsorbed. This is unlikely to be the case. During the course of a lifetime, there must be moments in which the overself looks out through our eyes, listens with our ears. Indeed, it may be that the overself is doing so all the time, but we are not consciously aware of it.

This brings up a second difficulty. Whatever the overself may be up to, something in the process of incarnation forces us, by and large, to identify with the current personality. Thus most of us live our lives as if we had only one life to live and remain in ignorance of any aspect of ourselves other than those personality factors which enable us to cope with day by day existence.

It seems reasonable to suggest that when the overself creates a new personality seed for incarnation, it attempts to incorporate the lessons learned from previous lives. Sometimes it is stunningly successful as when a highly developed musical talent appeared in the child Mozart. More often it is not, for few of us would claim to be living up to the full potential of our present life, let alone the whole daisy chain of previous existences. But once we begin consciously to exercise far memory, a whole new set of factors enters the picture.

First, we seem to release destructive tensions. Such tensions, frequently unrecognized at any conscious level, are at best a barrier against serenity and happiness and at worst the root of serious illness. The process of release often has profound therapeutic effects, but even where these are absent, those who have achieved genuine recall of past lives are almost always more secure and effective in their present life.

Next, we create a channel between one life and another through which talents and skills may seep. Gerald Glaskin discovered that, following his Christos experiments, a long-standing writer's block disappeared and was replaced by an outpouring of creativity.

Recall of old skills is a more important development than it might superficially appear. Humanity's racial evolution has depended largely on the communication of skills. Language itself was the first great step forward. Prior to its development, an individual might stumble on a particular technique, but could communicate it only by example. With language, however, a far more formalized training was possible, allowing skills to be distributed quickly through a tribal grouping.

The invention of writing represented the next step forward. Descriptions of techniques could be handed down, thus permitting accumulated wisdom to pass from generation to generation.

In our present age, robots (of the types used in, for example, the motor industry) provide a new means of recording skills for posterity. Machines mimic craftspeople and will continue to do so flawlessly for as long as we maintain them. But while robots preserve skills, they also freeze them. A human worker will typically develop and improve: a robot remains the same forever.

Far memory, by contrast, seems to have a real potential for insuring an individual's experience and skill do not die with the individual, but actually continue to grow and develop from one life to the next. This is an exciting prospect indeed when viewed on a collective basis. Far memory does something else as well — possibly the most important thing of all. It tends increasingly to shift one's personal identification from the impermanent personality to the overself. The combined effect of these various factors is to stimulate personal evolution to a marked degree.

Lesson Twelve

With this lesson, you have reached the end of your course and the beginning of what might, hopefully, become a long-term study. By now, you should have begun to accumulate far memory material and you are certainly equipped with the tools to continue to do so.

In so far as this material pertains to your own past lives, you should, after validation, subject it to careful analysis and scrutiny. In particular, look for patterns which repeat from life to life, or instances in past lives which help you understand this one. Try to trace the influences which reach from one link of the daisy chain to another.

When you have found them, pause a moment to consider whether they have a positve or negative effect on your wellbeing and personal growth . . . and if negative, see what you can do to make a change. For however often a pattern may repeat, there is nothing in the whole of reincarnation research to suggest you are immutably bound by it.

This is your practical work for the final lesson. It may take you the rest of your life to complete it.

Appendix I.

Troubleshooting: An A,B,C of Potential Problems in Reincarnation Research

Murphy's Law states that if anything can go wrong, it *will* go wrong.

In two decades and more of reincarnation research, I must have come across just about everything that *could* go wrong. If you persevere with your own research, it seems likely that, sooner or later, you may stir up a little trouble too.

When it happens, this appendix may help. I have listed — in alphabetical order — some of the more commonplace problems associated with the investigation of past lives. I certainly don't guarantee all, or even any, of the following disasters will come your way, but if one does, you will at least find a word of advice on how to tackle the problem.

Avoidance

Problem

It will sometimes happen that an individual, faced with personally conclusive proof that he or she has lived before, will seek to avoid the implications of the realization. Typical symptoms of avoidance are:

a) Denial of the experience or evidence that led to the proof. This can actually take the form of selective amnesia, forgetting details of the experience, then eventually forgetting the experience was ever undergone.

b) Abrupt abandonment of reincarnation research. Curiously, this course is most often taken when a great deal of enthusiasm about the research was originally present.

c) Refusal to discuss reincarnation theory or research. The individual may become angry or otherwise disturbed if attempts are made to force a discussion.

d) Temporary withdrawal from social activity. The degree of withdrawal can vary widely from a sort of brooding vagueness to actual physical isolation.

Action

It is important to realize these symptoms are all ways of attempting to deal with information and experiences which, by their nature, have an extremely disruptive effect on the sort of personal philosophy usually developed by a Western upbringing. Not all of them are negative. Abandonment of research, refusal to discuss the problem and a brooding withdrawal from social activities can all be an attempt to come to terms with the original experience. Even denial, the most troublesome response, may not necessarily be a permanent condition.

However avoidance is presented, the best action is inaction. No amount of rational argument or emotional appeal is likely to change the mind of an individual so shocked to discover the reality of reincarnation that he or she had begun to run from it. But given enough time (and a little understanding), there is a reasonable chance the individual may have sufficient intellectual honesty to work through the difficulty and integrate the new information.

Behavioural Abnormalities

Problem

Sudden changes in normal behaviour patterns may arise following successful reincarnation research. Although these are seldom extreme, they can be worrying to family and friends. The individual concerned is often described as 'different' or 'not himself'.

Action

The term *abnormality* tends, unfortunately, to suggest an illness or pathology, whereas in this case, it is almost always nothing of the sort. Behaviour changes can arise from:

a) Inability to integrate the evidence of a past life. (*See* **Avoidance**.)

b) A revival of past life patterns.

In the first instance, there is little that can be done except wait. Most individuals eventually manage to integrate new experiences, however shattering they may have been found initially.

The second instance is a little more difficult, since any action contemplated must depend on the actual nature of the behaviour changes. It is entirely possible

— indeed, in my experience, quite usual — for past-life recall to change behaviour patterns for the better. This is obviously something to be welcomed.

Neutral changes — actions that are simply *different* from past behaviour, but not disruptive or antisocial — are usually best accepted and left alone. Change is an integral part of the human condition and far memory sometimes does no more than accelerate the natural process.

Where behaviour patterns change for the worse, discussion is called for. Specifically, you should try to convince the individual that behaviour appropriate to a past life is not necessarily appropriate to his current existence. Make the point that the thrust of personal evolution must be towards progress, not a simple repetition of past patterns.

Negative changes of this type are difficult to cope with, especially in someone who is, or was, emotionally close, but it is some consolation to know that behavioural abnormalities arising out of reincarnation research tend to be short-lived.

Breakdown

See **Nervous Breakdown.**

Depression

Problem

Depression manifests as feelings of hopelessness, emptiness and sadness, usually resulting in reduced desire to communicate or socialize. The individual suffering from depression will often consider his or her personal worth to be low. In extreme cases, there can be a breakdown in the individual's ability to function effectively, leading to severe problems in the home and at work.

Action

A full-blown depression should never be taken lightly, whatever its cause. If it persists, medical help should be sought. In the case of depression arising out of reincarnation research, there is an additional problem in that few doctors, and fewer psychiatrists, accept the reality of past-life recall and may consequently be tempted to view reincarnation research experiences as part of an overall pathology.

The ideal solution is to find a practitioner with an interest or belief in reincarnation research. They do exist, as you will have noted earlier in this book, but are far less common in Britain, for example, than the United States — and not exactly *very* common even there.

Failing the ideal, it may be possible to alleviate the symptoms (and perhaps even cure the disease completely) by persuading the individual concerned to discuss openly and freely those past-life experiences that triggered the depression. It is important to maintain a non-judgemental attitude during this process, and equally important to point out that a past life is just that — something *past*. What happened then should not be allowed to cast a negative shadow over one's present existence.

Ego Inflation

Problem

This is a problem all too prevalent among certain types of occultist interested in reincarnation. It manifests in an exaggerated sense of self-importance, usually based on far memory of a life as a king, queen, priest, priestess or other powerful individual. Individuals suffering from ego inflation are usually the bores of reincarnation research, although in situations where inflation is accompanied by personal charisma, the individual can sometimes persuade others to accept his inflated opinion of himself and gather a nucleus of followers.

Action

First, it is important to realize that ego inflation is not something that only happens to other people. It can happen to you (and even me!) just as easily, especially in the heady hothouse atmosphere of reincarnation recall. It is also important to recognize that not all examples of ego inflation are grossly exaggerated. In other words, there are degrees of the problem.

Inflation is particularly difficult to deal with, since the individual concerned has little motive to do anything positive about the condition. For most sufferers, the first line of defence is to deny the disease completely, vigorously maintaining that they are, in fact, humble and modest individuals. It is, however, their actions rather than their claims which point to the problem.

It is probably fair to say that should you suspect ego inflation in your own character, you have a far better chance of doing something about it than if you spot the problem in someone else.

The first step is to take a long, hard and highly suspicious look at the example of far memory which triggered the inflation. However vivid your recall, it is statistically unlikely that you really were either Cleopatra or Julius Caesar. Re-examine the evidence with genuine cynicism and you may well find the foundations of your inflation collapse.

An absolute rule of reincarnation research is: *Be particularly suspicious of any far memory which tends to raise your sense of self-importance.* Sometimes this is fairly easy. If you memory is of a life in a position of power, or of a known (hence famous) historical personality, the possibility of inflation is obvious. But it can also be there in far more subtle guise. Recall of a life as an unknown pauper might also form the basis of ego inflation (when, for example, you consider yourself spiritually elevated because of it).

A useful approach is to try to see far memory in its own historical context. Distance lends enchantment, and enchantment can, sometimes, lead to ego inflation. But when a life is seen in context, it loses much of its glamour. The medieval merchant is today's small shopkeeper. The brave barbarian warrior equates to an army Private. The oriental scribe did no more than a modern typist. The application of context in this way has a distinctly deflationary effect.

Persuading others to deflate is usually a thankless task. You are probably best advised to leave them alone and concentrate on avoiding any temptation to become drawn into their fantasies.

Eroticism

Problem

This is a specific behavioural change (*see* **Behavioural Abnormalities**) in which previously suppressed sexual energies are released and channelled into new forms of expression.

Action

This problem may not be directly related to the experience of far memory at all. If you are experimenting with hypnosis in relation to reincarnation research, the possibility of triggering an erotic response in a subject is always there — but the response, when it arises, is frequently rooted in the act of hypnosis itself, not the regression memories produced.

The linkage between erotic response and hypnosis is often ignored in the textbooks, but any experienced hypnotist is likely to have come across it at some time. It is not inevitable, not even particularly common, but it can, and does, arise sometimes when hypnotist and subject are of different sexes.

Hypnosis is an intimate procedure in which the subject enters a relaxed, free-floating state in which the importance of the hypnotist is temporarily exaggerated. If there is any physical attraction between the two, the conditions are right for it to find overt expression.

If you are the hypnotic subject, recognizing the mechanics of the situation may help you avoid embarrassing comments or actions. If you are the hypnotist on the receiving end of an erotic suggestion, the simplest solution is to treat it lightly, recognizing that it is usually no more than a reflection of the immediate situation rather than anything deeper.

Eroticism arising out of far memory can be more far-reaching and consequently more troublesome. Sexual *mores* vary considerably with the country and the century. At any given time, our current patterns of sexual behaviour seem as normal as the laws of nature and it is easy to form the unthinking conclusion that the way we behave and believe are absolutes. Against this background, an experience of far memory involving substantially different *mores* can be shattering.

One young woman of my acquaintance put it succinctly: 'If I found I had been a prostitute in a past life, I don't think I would ever view men in the same light again.'

If a release of libido triggered by far memory of different sexual *mores* proves troublesome, a good way to tackle the problem is to place the new behaviour problem in context (a technique advocated for several other problems). Try to see that what was appropriate behaviour in one time and place is not necessarily appropriate behaviour now. Remembering a life as a cave-dweller is no excuse for wearing skins and carrying a club to work today. Adopting the sexual morality of an earlier age is usually just as silly.

Fear

See **Panic Attacks.**

'Going Lilac'

Problem

I am indebted to Margaret O'Donnell for the phrases *lilac people* and *going lilac.* She had noted that a certain type of individual with esoteric interests (including, I am sorry to say, reincarnation research) inclined towards vagueness, impracticality, histrionics, a saccharin 'spirituality' and a liking for diaphanous robes coloured lilac. Enough of these characteristics and you qualify as a lilac person, even without the robes.

Action

If a friend or colleague threatens to 'go lilac' as the result of reincarnation research, the simplest solution is to withdraw all support systems. A lilac person is typically so divorced from everyday reality that they survive comfortably only with assistance from their more practical — and often long-suffering — relatives and friends. Once this support is withdrawn, they will normally show a suprising talent for looking after themselves and, while it may take a little while, lilac attitudes will eventually crumble.

The approach may seem hard-hearted, but ultimately far memory is useful only in that it permits us to learn from our past, not to lock ourselves into it.

Headache

Problem

If hypnosis is used in reincarnation research, headaches can sometimes (rarely) occur when the subject emerges from the trance state.

Action

This problem is most often due to incorrect hypnotic technique rather than any reaction to the research. Inexperienced hypnotists sometimes terminate a trance sessions with suggestions such as 'You will have no pain' or 'You will not have a headache'. Suggestions of this type are often counterproductive. The unconscious mind of the subject (which is the target of the suggestion) can all too easily fail to hear the negative included in the sentence. As a result, the suggestion becomes 'You will have pain' or 'You will have a headache'. Ever obliging, the unconscious mind complies and the headache results.

The simplest way to deal with the problem is to ensure *all* hypnotic suggestions are couched in *positive* terms. Phrases like 'You will awaken feeling well, feeling happy, feeling on top of the world . . .' etc. ensure that the subject enjoys sensations of well-being when awakened, without the dangers of inadvertent headache triggers.

See also **Migraine.**

Irritability

Problem

Bouts of unusual irritability can occur in reincarnation research subjects. These are far from commonplace, but where they do occur, they can vary from mild annoyance to bursts of fury.

Action

This problem can arise from either of two causes. The first is the impact of far memory on the subject's philosophical or religious belief structures. The second is the fact that the experience of far memory almost always involves an upsurge of emotional energy, which can sometimes create friction within the personality.

In either case, the best course is to ignore the bad temper, avoid provocation and wait. The problem is seldom serious and unlikely to last long.

See also **Philosophy Conflict.**

Life Scripts

Problem

The term *life script* is drawn from Transactional Analysis (TA) and refers to the broad, overall pattern of a patient's life. Transactional analysts have noted certain patients unconsciously organize their lives to fall into line with a predetermined pattern which can, in some cases, be negative or even destructive. It is as if they were determined to follow a hidden script which ensured their lives ended in a particular way.

Reincarnation research will sometimes prompt a type of behavioural abnormality (*see* **Behavioural Abnormalities**) in which the subject begins to use the *overall* pattern of a previous life as the basis of a script for this one. If the previous life ended in disaster, then the subject works to ensure this life too ends the same way. If the previous life showed a pattern of emotional problems, then the subject begins to develop the same pattern now. And so on.

Action

The adoption of a prior life script is one of the most potentially troublesome aspects of reincarnation research. It is *not* a common problem, but where it arises, it can be tricky to deal with and highly destructive, both to the individual concerned and those around him or her.

A major step towards coping with this sort of situation is the development of an understanding of its mechanics. Study of TA would be of real value — and there are several very readable expositions of this psychiatric system on the market. In the interim, the following guidelines may be of help.

First, it is important to recognize that the dynamic of a script is *unconscious*. That is to say, the individual concerned does not realize he or she is manipulating his or her own life to conform to a predetermined pattern. Indeed, if the suggestion is made that a script is being followed, the individual will typically deny this — often vehemently or angrily. Next, while a script may ultimately be destructive (some end in suicide) it will always carry certain short-term benefits for the individual who follows it.

Such benefits may be subtle — a sense of purpose, the ability to avoid decision making etc. — but they will be there; and the tenacity with which a script is normally followed tends to be proportional to the importance of the benefits achieved.

A life script generated by the experience of far memory *can* be treated successfully by TA, but it differs in its fundamentals from the sort of pathological life script created by an individual to satisfy the emotional needs of the present life. Where reincarnation plays a part in the establishment of a life script, it is almost always a question of mimicry based on an inflated impression of the previous life.

Basically, what it comes down to is this: A subject triggers memories of a past life during the course of reincarnation research. This life will obviously be in a different time and may be in a different country, possibly a distant and exotic country. Distance, as the proverb says, lends enchantment, so that the remembered life may well seem a great deal more glamorous, exciting and fulfilling than the present day existence. Given that the individual is sufficiently desperate, the unconscious may seek to rectify the deficiencies of the present life by driving the individual to follow the pattern of the past life — in essence rerunning the previous script.

There are obvious drawbacks to such a development. However objectively successful or important a past life may have been, its pattern is relevant only to its own time and place. Behaviour which led to fame and fortune in, for example, Ancient Rome, would be more likely to get you locked up today.

Fortunately, the very weakness of a reincarnatory life script makes it a little easier to deal with than a script created by the unconscious as a direct result of current problems. Current problems remain, so any attempt to demolish the life script involves the abandonment of a solution, however destructive that solution may have been. A reincarnatory life script is seldom created on any firmer foundation than fascination with the earlier life. Because of this, a conscious realization that a script is being followed, coupled with the realization that it is no longer an *appropriate* script, is often enough to release the individual.

Where the situation becomes really difficult is where the reincarnatory script coincidentally meets current emotional needs. In such situations, you have all the troublesome dynamics of an orthodox transactional life script added to the fascination with a past life. Often the only answer is to seek professional assistance.

Marital Conflicts

Problem

Reincarnation research is qualitatively different from, for example, an interest in archaeology or history, in that it tends to be viewed in emotional terms. Because of this, individuals engaged in reincarnation research will sometimes find themselves at odds with their spouses because of it.

Action

Marital problems triggered by reincarnation research do not always present themselves openly. Often the first hint of trouble is an angry disagreement about some totally unconnected matter. In such circumstances, it is vitally important to bring the real cause into the open. This can only be done if both partners are willing to tackle their disagreements with patience and insight. Only when agreement has been reached about the real root of the problem, does the possibility of finding a solution arise.

Generally speaking, marital problems arise in this sphere when one partner is interested in the research and the other is not. In such situations, it is not uncommon for the second partner to be frightened or disturbed by the other's activities. Even simple disinterest can lead to disagreement, but these are generally about priorities and can usually be resolved fairly easily given flexibility and goodwill on both sides.

Where a partner is frightened or disturbed by reincarnation research, however, the situation becomes considerably more difficult. Fear reactions should never be underestimated. The first step in dealing with the situation is to attempt to understand the fear, to put yourself in the other partner's place and see the research from his or her viewpoint.

Those unfamiliar with the whole field of reincarnation may see it as mysterious, sinister and occult, consequently fearing for the safety of the researcher. They may also fear alienation from their partner, whose attention is directed into these strange channels.

It is worth remembering that such fears are not always groundless — this entire appendix is based on the principle that reincarnation research can create problems. It is also worth remembering that they are based on a genuine interest in and concern for the researcher.

Against this background, the most likely solution to the problem might be found in a patient attempt to explain the techniques and results of the research to the worried partner. Nothing is more frightening than the unknown, so any light shed on the research activities is likely to diminish the fear at least a little. But the keynote is patience. The worried partner may well resist learning about the research and a good deal of time may be needed to resolve the difficulties. Maintain an open, frank attitude throughout, hide nothing about the research and its findings, keep patience and, if necessary, show willingness to abandon research — at least temporarily — as a goodwill gesture.

See also **Relationship Problems.**

Migraine

Problem

Migraine is a particularly violent form of headache which sometimes affects only one side of the head and is frequently accompanied by nausea, vomiting and eye problems such as flashing lights and blank spots in the field of vision.

The immediate cause of the problem is dilation of the blood vessels of the brain, but the condition is often related to stress and/or food allergies, the most common triggers being chocolate, coffee and cheese. There is some suggestion that liver/gall-bladder functions may also be involved in some cases.

A number of researchers have postulated a past life connection with migraine.

Action

Within the framework of the past life postulate, migraine is seen as a signal that far memories are trying to push their way into consciousness — a painful version of the recurring dream. If this is so, then an investigation into your past lives should theoretically, alleviate the condition.

If it does not, migraine can often be controlled by means of vitamin therapy (regular supplements of Vitamin B complex) and/or relaxation. Acupuncture has a good success rate in curing the problem completely.

Obsession

Problem

There are two versions of this problem. One is an obsession by the research subject with the details of a previous life, sometimes manifesting in an attempt to relive past patterns (*see* **Life Scripts**), sometimes in an unhealthy interest in the manners and/or fashions of the past-life period. The other is a sort of takeover by the past-life personality, which seems to reach into the present life — a process bordering on possession.

Action

An interest in the time and country of a past life recalled through far memory is perfectly normal, even commonplace. There are few reincarnation researchers who have not succumbed at some stage to the temptation to collect a few artefacts from a past-life period. A problem really only arises when this is carried to extreme and the individual is surrounded by bric-a-brac from the period or affects its fashions in the present day.

If you find yourself sliding uncomfortably in this direction, it is worth asking yourself *why* you seek to escape from the present day, since retreat from current problems is almost always a factor in the development. Once you recognize *consciously* what you are doing, it is usually a simple enough matter to take yourself in hand. Retreat does not, after all, solve the problems and any attempt to live in the distant past (which, whatever your links, is now long dead) must ultimately come to nothing.

The second form of obsession is a good deal less common and a great deal more dangerous. The mechanics of the situation are intricate and difficult to understand. As a starting point, you should clearly recognize that the personality you recall from a previous life *no longer exists*. It is not some bizarre form of ghost with an existence outside yourself, but rather a dramatized memory.

This would seem to make possessive obsession impossible, but such is not the case. Dramatized memories have much in common with fictional characters — and fictional characters, as any novelist will confirm, take on a life of their own.

Quite how dramatic this phenomenon can be is underlined by the experience of a group from the Toronto Society for Psychical Research, who created a fictional ghost named Philip. Having settled on a historical period in which he was supposed to have lived, they dreamed up a detailed life history for him, which included descriptions of his appearance, romantic liaisons and death. When the creative process was complete, Philip began to manifest at seances held by the group, producing raps and engaging in mediumistic communication. He was able to give accurate details of his historical environment *of which members of the group were not consciously aware*. He also proved himself perfectly capable of *adding to* the life history the group had created for him.

Although the experiment was undertaken in the name of psychical research, it obviously has a great deal of importance in the field of psychology. Clearly, it is possible for the human mind to create entities which, while mental constructs, have a real or pseudo objectivity.

In this context, it may be appropriate to mention again the experience of Madame Alexandra David-Neel, the French explorer who was the only European woman ever to become a Tibetan Lama. During her years in Tibet, Madame David-Neel stumbled on the mystical technique of *tulpa* creation whereby, so the Tibetans claimed, an entity might be visualized with such force that it became real. Madame David-Neel tried the technique and discovered it worked. The hooded monk-like figure she created became first a personal hallucination, then something which was seen by others in the camp. Eventually, to her extreme discomfort, it broke away from her control.

Against this background, it can sometimes happen that a past-life personality begins to act a little like Madame David-Neel's *tulpa*. In such circumstances, it can have a powerful possessive quality.

It is possible, but not entirely advisable, to deal with the problem using orthodox psychiatric methods — the inadvisability stemming from the difficulty in finding a competent psychiatrist who sympathizes with reincarnation research. A better way is to recognize the dynamics of what is happening. A past-life personality which seems to develop a life of its own, does so only because you have spent too much time visualizing it and imagining its activities. You can literally starve it to death by refusing to play the game any longer and turning your attention purposefully elsewhere. (A temporary break from reincarnation research is obviously recommended.)

An alternative approach, more difficult to undertake but with a substantially more satisfying outcome, is to recognize that the personality is ultimately an aspect of your *self*, built up during a past life and reinforced by your attention during this one. As an aspect of your self, it can be *absorbed into* your self by an effort of will. This approach is not, however, recommended unless you are certain your present personality is sound, strong and well-balanced.

Panic Attacks

Problem

Those engaged in the personal development of far memory will sometimes find themselves prey to panic attacks, which present fear symptoms — often extreme — unrelated to any current cause.

Action

Panic attacks are uncomfortable in the extreme and can lead to additional symptoms such as depression if they cannot be overcome. Typically, such attacks will strike without warning, often late at night or in the early hours of the morning. Their symptomology can include sweating, palpitations and severe muscle tension amounting at times to rigidity. Panic attacks involve (among other factors) an over-production of adrenaline in the body and can lead to feelings of exhaustion if a series of attacks continues over a prolonged period.

When related to reincarnation research, the attacks usually spring from:

a) An actual or impending breakdown of philosophical or religious beliefs under the impact of far memory.

b) The approach of a buried trauma within the research context.

If the first of these factors is suspected, see the sections of the appendix entitled **Philosophy Conflict** and **Religious Conflict.**

The second factor requires a little explanation. Past-life research is a process similar in many respects to psychoanalysis in that areas of the psyche previously hidden from consciousness are explored. And just as psychoanalysis can unearth a buried trauma, so too can reincarnation research.

Any trauma is, by definition, painful. Some traumas — the death of a loved one, sexual assault by a siblng. the moment of birth or, in reincarnation research, the experience of personal death — can be too painful to be borne by the conscious mind. When such a trauma arises, the mind will typically work hard to forget it. But memory cannot be destroyed. Instead it is *pushed down* into the unconscious areas of the mind and — if particularly painful — surrounded by guardian elements which divert attention away if they is any danger of its being approached again.

The process is not pathological. On the contrary, it is an important part of mental hygiene. But no process can function flawlessly in all circumstances and situations do arise in which the emotional charge associated with the memory is so powerful that the trauma festers, so to speak, below the threshold of consciousness, creating neurotic symptoms and influencing the life pattern to considerable detriment. In such a case, the only real answer is to retrieve the buried memory and attempt to integrate its contents into consciousness — something far from easy.

A festering trauma is more often associated with the present life than with any past existence. While past life traumas *can* give trouble, most are so well buried that they never see the light of consciousness . . . unless, that is, you disturb them in the course of reincarnation research.

An illustration will make this easier to understand. Assume for a moment you had a past life in which you were tortured and burned by the Spanish Inquisition. In order to protect you from the horror of the experience, your mind would take great care to bury the memories, and in normal circumstances, this trauma would be too well hidden to cause you any trouble. But in the course of reincarnation research, it is entirely possible that you could stumble on the life in question, entirely by accident.

It is unlikely that you would find yourself in the midst of the horror. The mind's defences can cope reasonably well even with the techniques of reincarnation research. But as you continue to explore the life, you must sooner or later find yourself approaching the critical period. And in order to divert you from the horror, your unconscious mind would generate panic attacks — a warning signal indicating that you are moving too close to something with which your conscious mind may not be able to cope.

When such a signal sounds, you have the option to ignore it. If you press on quickly with your research and unearth the traumatic experience, there is an excellent chance that the discharge of associated emotions will put an end to your panic problems. Once the trauma has been faced and its contents integrated into consciousness, the panic attacks should disappear. But this course of action has its dangers. The unconscious mind does not send out warning signals lightly, so that there is always a risk that reliving the buried trauma will generate serious emotional problems — the very situation, in short, that the warnings were constructed in order to avoid.

Like many situations in life, this one comes down to a trade-off. You need to weigh the risks involved against the promised returns. If you can successfully integrate the trauma into consciousness, your panic attacks should disappear. But equally, if you decide to take the safer course and avoid probing any further into the life in question, then the panic attacks should also disappear once your decision is made.

Philosophy Conflict

Problem

The findings of reincarnation research can run contrary to the particular world picture held by the individual involved.

Action

This problem is similar in certain respects to that of **Religious Conflict** and can be troublesome if the personality involved is inflexible in nature.

Broadly speaking, all of us develop a particular way of looking at the world, based on a series of (largely unquestioned) assumptions. We may not think of this as our personal philosophy, but it is. Western culture tends to produce personal philosophies which have little place for the idea of reincarnation. We try not to think of death at all, but when we do, there is a tendency to view it as an ending or, if we are religiously inclined, as the beginning of a new phase in some other reality — heaven or hell, depending on our level of self-confidence.

Ideas of this type form the basis of our thoughts and actions and are all the more potent because they are bedrock assumptions seldom questioned consciously. Reincarnation research, however, can shatter such assumptions brutally, leaving the individual with a feeling of fear and vulnerability. An emotional conflict frequently sets in, providing an extremely painful experience until resolved.

There is no easy answer to this problem. No one enjoys the feelings which arise when a personal philosophy is disturbed. Some actually find it so painful that they will elect to deny the research experience rather than revise their cherished assumptions.

Intellectual honesty is a help, since it is obviously worthless to cling to ideas superseded by experience. But the problem itself is essentially emotional and can only be worked through slowly and painfully. Try to remember that the results of your research will not necessarily confound your entire philosophy — only certain aspects of it. Examine you assumptions carefully, retaining those which still hold up and only abandoning those you can no longer accept in all honesty. With patience, you will construct a new philosophy on sounder foundations than the first.

Psi Phenomena

Problem

Psi phenomena — the development of talents like telepathy, clairvoyance or psychokinesis — may appear during the course of reincarnation research.

Action

Psi phenomena are as rare in reincarnation research as they are everywhere else. But they can and do occur in certain circumstances. Fortunately these circumstances are quite clearly defined, so that a knowledge of them can provide advance warning of possible developments.

During reincarnation research, psi phenomena are likely to arise when — and only when — the past life under investigation has itself a psi component. You might, for example, recall a past life as a witch (a suprisingly large number of researchers do) or as a medium or priest with particular abilities. Once the link has been formed, it is possible — although by no means inevitable — that you will experience a resurgence of the old ability in the present life.

The mechanics of the situation are quite straightforward. However it may appear, reincarnation research is actually the reawakening of buried memories. If, at one stage of your evolution, you enjoyed a particular psychic talent, then the reawakening of the memory of that talent will sometimes allow you to use it again. The fact that remembering does not *automatically* give you access to the former talent only underlines the complexity of talent in general and psychical talent in particular.

If technique is an important component in the talent, then memory will tend to revive the talent itself — provided you awaken memories of the technique and not merely the fact that you once had the talent. But many psi talents rely on much more than technique. You might, for example, require a particular physical or emotional disposition which no longer forms a part of your individuality. In such cases, no amount of far memory will regenerate the psi ability.

For some people, a psychic talent can be frightening, especially one that arrives unexpectedly and unannounced during the course of reincarnation research. Unfortunately, once such a talent has been awakened, it is virtually impossible to obliterate. (Once you learn how to ride a bicycle, you tend to be able to do it to your dying day, however long it has been since you last went near one.) But you can, of course, elect to ignore it.

Occasionally, the talent will manifest in an uncontrolled form, popping up when you least expect it or, worse, when you least want it. Uncontrolled psychism is seldom actually dangerous, but it can be extremely uncomfortable. If you find yourself in this situation, it could be of benefit to take training to bring the talent under control.

Such training is currently available within the Spiritualist movement, the Witch Cult and many esoteric schools, but do take care to use discrimination in selecting your mentors, since there are still fools and rogues in all these movements. The training itself is nothing more occult than the establishment of a series of conditioned reflexes (of the type Pavlov discovered when he carried out his famous experiment with dogs). They may be presented in odd guises, but they remain conditioned reflexes just the same.

Religious Conflict

Problem

The findings of reincarnation research can run contrary to the religious beliefs of the individual involved.

Action

This problem is similar to that of **Philosophy Conflict,** but tends to be substantially more troublesome.

Religious beliefs differ from personal philosophy in that the latter is usually founded to some extent on direct personal experience of the world, while religious beliefs are largely *instilled*. Once instilled, usually during childhood, they tend to be reinforced by our emotions and needs and are often immune to any buffeting from experience. Indeed, they may well be kept in a totaly separate mental compartment from the rest of our day-to-day experience.

Without wishing to comment on the validity of any religious doctrine, it is plain that the structure of an individual's religious beliefs can be of considerable — and sometimes supreme — importance to that individual's emotional and psychological well-being. Thus anything which conflicts with religious belief can, in certain circumstances, be a destructive force.

While reincarnation research is concerned with fact and experience, it obviously operates within an area which overlaps the metaphysical. In other words, the findings of reincarnation research can sometimes force us into a reevaluation of our religious beliefs.

Such a position is seldom comfortable and can sometimes be quite shattering to the individual concerned. Many religious doctrines are irrational (a word not used in any pejorative sense) and survive by being held separate from the mind's more rational constructs. But reincarnation research will often push the two together, in that it forces the individual to examine his or her belief structures in the light of new personal experience.

As with philosophy conflict, it sometimes happens that the belief structures can only survive at the price of denying experience. The resultant conflict is extreme and complicated dramatically by the emotional factors inherent in religion.

There is no easy way out of this dilemma. Obviously a religious belief system which *already* supports the concept of reincarnation will create few difficulties. Nor will a system with nothing to say about the afterlife, since reincarnation can be integrated into it without difficulty. But most modern interpretations of Western religions leave no room at all for reincarnation. Christianity, for example, promises physical resurrection at an unspecified future date, following the Second Coming of Christ; Islam promises a post-mortem Paradise of sloe-eyed virgins for its male adherents; Judaism is generally far more concerned with this world than the next, but does have a doctrine of a rather grim afterlife in a world of colourless shades.

How can one reconcile these teachings with an experience of far memory? The simple answer is that you cannot. You are forced into a situation where you modify your belief structure or ignore your experience.

Regrettably, it is in the nature of religious structures that they resist modification. Indeed, fundamentalists of almost every religion tend to argue that any modification is sinful and must be fought forcefully. And even those who are far from fundamentalist in their beliefs will generally feel extremely uncomfortable with any attempt to amend the structures they currently hold.

As always, the ultimate choice must be left to the individual. If your religion is more precious, more important to you than truth and experience, then the solution to your problem lies in the abandonment of reincarnation research and the vigorous denial of any far memory experience you may have had. In this way, you will protect your peace of mind and ensure, by and large, that you bring a stop to your personal evolution. If, however, you are prepared to allow experience to modify belief, then you are undoubtedly faced with a difficult and painful task in changing your belief structure. Not alone will you have to fight your own emotional needs, but you may well come under pressure from your peers, who will seldom take kindly to your modification of a belief system they may well share.

Two factors which may be of help if you follow the Christian religion are:

a) The percentage of practising Christians who manage to encompass reincarnation into their belief structures.

b) The body of evidence which suggests reincarnation was an early tenet of Church doctrine and may well have been taught by Christ himself.

On the first point, a poll taken by Gallup in 1982 showed 25 per cent of

American Catholics, 26 per cent of Methodists and 21 per cent of all other Protestants accepted the doctrine of reincarnation, however uneasily it might rest with the remainder of their beliefs. Given, therefore, that 23 per cent of all American adults, irrespective of religious persuasion, believe in reincarnation (and the figure is unlikely to be all that much different in other Christian countries), you may at least take comfort in the fact that you are not alone.

The second point, relating to evidence of early Christian — and, indeed, Jewish — belief in reincarnation, is one that would repay careful personal investigation. It is a complex area, open to a multiplicity of interpretations, and only a few pointers can be given here. A good place to start your investigation might be the Bible, which does contain a number of statements directly or indirectly suggestive of a belief in reincarnation.

Old Testament references to Jacob and Esau contain several mentions of rebirth, while the prayer of Moses, quoted in Psalm 90: 3-5, refers to death in the following terms:

> 'Thou carriest them away as with a flood; they are as a sleep; in the morning they are like grass which groweth up.'

These words are reminiscent of pagan beliefs which hold there is a relationship between the seasonal growth/dormancy/regrowth cycle of plants and a supposed birth/death/rebirth cycle in humanity.

The New Testament contains passages with even clearer implications for a belief in reincarnation. In Matthew 10, for example, Christ explicitly identifies John the Baptist as Elijah reborn, and He does so more than once. In John 8:58, Jesus is quoted as saying, 'Before Abraham was, I am' — an affirmation of pre-birth existence. Other passages suggest, at least by implication, that such an existence was not unique to Jesus. John 9: 1-3 contains questions about a blind man, asking if his condition was caused by his own sin. Since the man was born blind, this could only mean sin *before birth*. Clearly the implication is that the disciples held a belief in pre-existence, and Jesus said nothing to suggest this was inaccurate.

In the final book of the Bible, Revelation 13:10, comes the blunt statement: 'He that leadeth into captivity shall go into captivity: he that killeth with the sword must be killed with the sword.' Although this might, of course, be interpreted as an admonition concerned with the establishment of a legal system (another version of the famous *Eye for an eye, tooth for a tooth* principle), an equally valid interpretation might be to suggest the words refer to *karma*, a system of cosmic balance inherent in Hindu and Buddhist ideas about reincarnation. If this interpretation is correct, then it follows that retribution must come in a future life since manifestly a good many soldiers (who 'killed with the sword') still manage to die peacefully in bed.

Outside of the accepted Canon, Gnostic scriptures contain even clearer references to Christ's belief in reincarnation. In the Pistis Sophia, for example, Jesus is quoted in the following words:

> 'Put not off from day to day and from cycle to cycle, in the belief that ye will succeed in obtaining the mysteries when ye return to the world in another cycle.'

Among the early Church fathers, the 3rd Century Origin had a firm belief in reincarnation, as his writings clearly show. That he was not alone in this belief is underlined by the fact that the Synod of Constantinople felt impelled to outlaw the doctrine in 529 AD. Following on its recommendations, the Emperor Justinian later issued fifteen anathemas, four of which were aimed at the notion of pre-existence and consequently at the doctrine of reincarnation. The strong tone of these declarations is indicated by this example:

> *'If anyone assert the fabulous preexistence of souls and shall assert the monstrous restoration which follows from it: let him be anathema.'*

Justinian submitted these anathemas to the Second Council of Constantinople in 553, and there they were adopted.

Relationship Problems

Problem

Belief in, or research into, reincarnation is seen as unusual or eccentric, in modern Western cultures and consequently can lead to relationship problems for those involved.

Action

Society as a whole tends towards conservatism — as a state of mind if not necessarily as a political doctrine. Anything which steps outside the norm is viewed with suspicion. People who engage in unusual pursuits (like reincarnation research) or hold to unusual doctrines (like a belief in the reality of reincarnation) tend to be treated as outsiders. Relationship problems consequently arise.

Perhaps the easiest way to avoid this problem is the use of discretion. Keeping your interests to yourself, or sharing them only with those whom you know to be in sympathy with your work, is an excellent way to steer clear of controversy. Nor does this approach necessarily involve dishonesty. Reincarnation is not, by and large, a commonplace topic of discussion — it falls well below soccer and politics as barber-shop subjects, for instance — and may never arise at all, even in the course of a long-term friendship.

In certain situations, however, this approach is impossible. The relationship may be too intimate for an important interest to be hidden (*see* **Marital Conflicts**), your activities in the area may be generally known, or the information may have been passed on by another. When this happens, it is often useful to give some reassurance by explaining what reincarnation research actually involves, on the principle that the unknown frequently appears far more sinister than it really is.

If this fails to alleviate the problem, you could try referring to some of the statistics quoted elsewhere in this appendix (*see* **Religious Conflict**) which suggest almost a quarter of the population shares your reincarnation interest. In the final analysis, however, you may need to ask yourself whether a relationship so weak that it might be seriously disturbed by your research activities is actually worth keeping.

Self-Deception

Problem

Those engaged in reincarnation research — and particularly those who strive to develop far memory — are constantly prone to the possibility of self deception. (*See also* **Going Lilac.**)

Action

The point has been made elsewhere in this Workbook that critics of reincarnation research perceive those who engage in it as remembering only lives of power, wealth and grandeur. While the reality differs considerably from this perception, there is sufficient truth in it to make it worth investigation. Certainly self-deception is rife in the field; and the danger of self-deception is constant even among the most conscientious researchers.

The first step in defeating self-deception is to accept that it could actually happen to you. This is by no means easy. Most of us like to believe we are immune to error and will go to great lengths to avoid seeing it in ourselves (whereas, of course, it is all too obvious in others). But we would not be human if we were not a prey to self-deception, and frank admission of the *possibility* will go a long way towards avoiding the *actuality*.

Once you admit the possibility, you have an opportunity of finding out where the real danger areas lie. This obviously involves a degree of self-knowledge. When dealing with this subject in the main body of the Workbook, I suggested you should remain suspicious of any life which tended to reinforce your sense of self-importance. But self-importance is something that may be based on a variety of factors. For some people, it is related to wealth; for others it is a matter of social position. But just as there is a form of reverse snobbery which clings blindly to working class values, so there are forms of self-importance which are founded on such laudable factors as charitable work, healing abilities, or a developed social conscience.

This takes the whole question of self-deception into a very subtle area indeed. No longer is it enough to become suspicious of a past life as a great leader, a famous personage or a multi-millionaire. You must also critically examine the evidence of any past life which tends to reinforce your sense of self-importance in *any* sphere. Ultimately, of course, the only way to guard absolutely against self-deception is to check *and recheck* your findings. However appealing details of a past life may be, they can only be considered valid if you are certain they are historically accurate.

Interestingly, research scientists (who are as much victims of self-deception as the rest of us . . . and know it) have discovered self-deception can very easily creep into verification procedures. If a particular result is important to you —

or even merely expected in advance — your unconscious mind can trick you into misreading a reference, miscalculating a statistic, or whatever, in order to support your preconception. This is why *rechecking* is as important as checking. Indeed, although it may seem to be overdoing caution, by far the best way to verify (or refute) a far memory is to have the historical details checked by someone other than yourself who is not involved in the remainder of the experiment.

Ties

Problem

The awakening of far memory can create ties to particular places and/or people which are not always appropriate to the present life.

Action

This one is difficult to avoid. If you reawaken details of a life in, for example, Ancient Egypt, it is perfectly natural to feel a desire to visit present day Egypt with the possibility of visiting some or all of the sites of your former existence. The temptation is harmless and the visit itself is unlikely to cause any problems — the experience of others suggests, in fact, that it is quite likely to provide a fulfilling adventure. It seldom, if ever, happens that researchers become sufficiently fixated on a particular place seriously to disrupt their normal behaviour patterns.

The same, unfortunately, cannot be said for reincarnatory fixations on *people*.

Real problems can arise when you feel yourself drawn to someone with whom you believe you shared a prior life. This is especially true of situations in which there was a romantic or emotional relationship in the previous existence. Old ties of this sort can be exceptionally strong; and to my certain knowledge there have been a considerable number of researchers who were unable to resist them, even at the cost of a broken marriage or career.

Should you find yourself faced with a situation of this type, it may be as well to ask yourself (as coolly as possible) whether or not you want to renew the old acquaintance . . . and if so, in what way. The fact that a particular couple were lovers in a previous life does not mean they are compelled to be lovers again in this one — they may be happier as friends or colleagues. They may, in fact, be happier never seeing one another again.

It is as well to remember in this context that relationships are seldom static, and reincarnatory relationships especially can run a whole gamut of change. My own research suggests it is by no means unusual for a couple to be husband and wife in one life, mother and daughter in another, close friends in a third. A host of emotional and sexual permutations is not merely possible, but actually likely across a spectrum of past lives. A realization of this fact can go a long way towards placing the reawakened emotional attraction in some form of perspective. But placing it in perspective is a long way from denying it altogether, a course which can lead to an emotional explosion.

One does not have to engage in reincarnation research for very many years to hear of marriages broken because one or other partner has revived memories of a past-life relationship with another man or woman. But there has always been a clear distinction between morality and *mores*, the latter being no more than the accepted customs and beliefs of a particular place and time. It is a sacred cow of Western culture that marriage should be considered sacrosanct (despite clear evidence that a great many people consider it to be nothing of the sort). Despite such conventional wisdom, it is plain that there are occasions when the break-up of a marriage is no bad thing. Certainly it can be infinitely preferable to the destructive dynamics associated with a thoroughly bad marriage.

All these factors should be taken into consideration when you make your decision on what to do about a revived relationship from the distant past.

Appendix II.

Reincarnation and the No-Soul Paradox in Buddhism

Oriental thought accepts reincarnation far more readily than the philosophies of the West. One of the great religions of the East, Buddhism, is actually based on the premise that the individual should strive to break free from the eternal Wheel of birth, death and rebirth represented by the reincarnation process.

For centuries, Buddhists have diligently practised techniques designed to help them reach *Nirvana*, that state of bliss and being from which it is no longer necessary to be reborn. As Buddhism spread from its native India, emphasis on reincarnation changed as the religion was modified to meet the social and psychological conditions prevalent in the countries where it took root.

In Japan, for example, Zen Buddhism placed emphasis on sudden, dramatic enlightenment, focused on the state of individual being here and now rather than in past or future lives. Tibetan Buddhism, by contrast, emphasized reincarnation almost more than any other aspect — to the extent of establishing a reincarnatory monarchy and a legal system which permitted debts contracted in this life to be repaid in the next.

But for all the importance of reincarnation to Buddhism, the root-stock of the religion contained a troublesome paradox. For among the Buddha's original teachings was the *anata* doctrine which stated categorically that the human soul — like so many other things viewed from the Buddhist viewpoint — was an illusion.

Within a religion founded on reincarnation, the no-soul doctrine has proven a bewilderment for generations of Buddhists, especially those in the West whose literal minds do not readily accept contradictions. While Buddhism answers such important questions as 'What must I do to be free?' or 'How shall I achieve salvation?', it is silent on the vital problem of '*What* reincarnates?' Indeed, Zen masters in particular have long had a tendency to look blankly at their pupils and insist '*Nothing* reincarnates'! If nothing reincarnates, then why should I strive to break free from the Wheel of birth, death and rebirth, the great cycle of reincarnation? In a Zen monastery, such a reasonable objection is likely to earn a whack about the head with a big stick.

For the millions who accept the enlightenment of Guatama Buddha, reincarnation research offers an interesting resolution of the paradox in that, as noted earlier in this Workbook, the concept of a soul (in the generally accepted sense of that term) is not absolutely necessary to a belief in reincarnation. The term *soul* can be interpreted in the sense of an immaterial vehicle, like the astral body of esoteric doctrine, or as the inner entity we experience as personality. In either case, it is plain that the soul does not long survive physical death. Far memory has little to say about ghost bodies and tends to reveal chains of personalities very different one from the other. Defined in these terms, the soul is thus *Maya* or illusion, an impermanent thing, exactly as the Buddhists claim.

What reincarnates is indeed *nothing* as the Zen masters affirm, for research tends to indicate it is wrong to view the process of reincarnation as a soul flitting from body to body, like a butterfly fluttering between flowers. Rather there seems to be a pre-existent entity which *reaches into* incarnation from time to time, creating a series of subtle vehicles — including a personality — in order to do so.

A much fuller discussion of this point is included in the body of the Workbook. Its relevance to this Appendix is the light it sheds on the techniques of Buddhist practice. If we view ourselves as pre-existent entities reaching occasionally into incarnation, then the Buddha's system for obtaining release from the Wheel, could be seen in actuality as a deepened realization of our essential nature.

The viewpoint throws fresh light on the ancient doctrine of *karma*, which, in its simplest form, reflects the Christian adage that you reap exactly what you sow. In its orthodox exposition, *karma* requires a whole cosmic machinery of justice to keep track of every individual's progress and peccadilloes and redress imbalances from life to life. It is a concept difficult to accept, especially since the operation of cosmic justice is conspicuous by its absence in any individual experience or study of history. But from the changed viewpoint, *karma* becomes personal rather than cosmic, a sort of learning by experience which drives the evolution of the entity. There is consequently no real imbalance, certainly no punishment or reward, but rather a continual movement towards greater and greater understanding, a fumbling towards the light.

Nothing reincarnates. We create certain temporary structures in order to learn and experience, but the essence of our being remains always outside incarnation. It is only from the limited viewpoint of such temporary vehicles as the personality that we imagine reincarnation to exist at all. What we remember as past lives should more accurately be described as previous experiences within an ongoing — and quite possibly eternal or timeless — existence.

As we grow to realize our true nature, as, in Buddhist terms, enlightenment is achieved, we are at long last presented with a fully conscious choice. We may remain what we are, sufficient unto ourselves, enjoying the state of pure being referred to in Buddhist scriptures as *Nirvana*, or we may elect to experience incarnation again, but with a fuller realization of the nature of the process. It is perhaps not so odd that the traditions of Buddhism encompass this choice. There are, so the doctrine maintain, two types of enlightenment — that of the Buddhas who accept the just reward of their efforts and cease to incarnate, and that of the Buddhas who elect to continue to incarnate in order to show the way to the mass of suffering humanity.

Certain insights are difficult to communicate in that they are inevitably filtered through the perceptions and preconceptions of the individual who receives them. This may have been the situation with Buddhist doctrine. While Guatama achieved enlightenment, his followers, almost by definition, are merely working their way towards it. It was their viewpoint of reincarnation which created the paradox of the *anata* doctrine, not the doctrine itself.

Index

Of further interest . . .

THE ASTRAL PROJECTION WORKBOOK

How to Achieve Out-of-Body Experiences

J.H. BRENNAN

If you've ever wanted to know how to enter another dimension, how to walk through walls, or how to achieve an out-of-body experience, *The Astral Projection Workbook* will teach you how.

Laid out in an easy-to-follow style, with useful practice exercises, this manual explains the theory behind two distinct forms of astral projection — and how to bring these states into being. The first half deals with etheric projection, which involves actually leaving the physical body and travelling considerable distances in a very short space of time. The second part looks closely at astral plane projection, transporting of the consciousness onto the Astral Plane, which is often achieved through visual imagination.

J.H. Brennan draws on a wide range of techniques, such as the use of astral doorways, pathworkings, divination and astral magic, and in order to ensure your astral travels are safe and stress-free he gives plenty of useful advice, including:

the laws of the astral planes

———— ★ ————

how to get back into your body

———— ★ ————

relaxation techniques

———— ★ ————

lucid dreaming

———— ★ ————

carefully-graded safe exercises

THE ESP WORKBOOK

How to Awaken and Use Your Psychic Powers

RODNEY DAVIES

Have you ever experienced *déjà vu*, seen a ghost, had a feeling of floating over your own body, or had a dream that later came true? If you have, you may have a strong aptitude for ESP. If you haven't, your psi abilities probably just need a nudge in the right direction — and this book will give it.

Extra-Sensory Perception is our sixth sense. It belongs to us all, and in this workbook Rodney Davies demonstrates how to explore and develop your inner powers. With an easy-to-follow style he presents an exhaustive insight into ESP phenomena and suggests simple tests in which you can exercise and influence your extra-sensory abilities.

In its fascinating and intriguing journey into the realm of ESP, this book will examine:

telepathy and clairvoyance

———— ★ ————

precognition and retrocognition

———— ★ ————

dowsing and psychometry

———— ★ ————

crystal-gazing and hypnotism

———— ★ ————

psychokinesis and astral projection

———— ★ ————

animal ESP and life after death